Common C Functions

Kim Jon Brand

Que Corporation
Indianapolis

Library of Congress Catalog No.: LC 84-61392
ISBN 0-88022-1069-4

Editorial Director
David F. Noble, Ph.D.

Editor
Virginia Noble, M.L.S.

Technical Editor
Chris DeVoney

Dedication

To my wife, Beth Ann Brand,
and to Clara Ann and Adam,
for their patience and training
on far more important subjects than C

Composed in Megaron by
Que Corporation

Printed and bound by
George Banta Co., Inc.

Cover designed by
Listenberger Design Associates

About the Author

Kim Jon Brand

Mr. Brand received a B.S. degree in mechanical engineering technology from Purdue University in 1975. For three years he worked in marketing at Union Carbide and later served as a systems/software expert for DY-4 Systems. Having formed two companies, Mr. Brand has acquired wide experience in communications, programming, finance, and systems consulting. He cofounded XYZ Electronics, Inc., which introduced three successful products into the industrial board-level market.

Currently, Mr. Brand does private consulting for a variety of companies and associations. His software-related activities include operating system and application package design and implementation.

Table of Contents

Trademark Acknowledgments

Recommended Reading

/c. Indianapolis, Ind.: Que Corporation. Published monthly.

C Users' Group Newsletter. Yates Center, Kans.: C Users' Group. Published monthly.

Dr. Dobb's Journal. Palo Alto, Calif.: M&T Publishing Company. Published monthly.

Feuer, Alan R. *The C Puzzle Book.* Englewood Cliffs, N.J.: Prentice-Hall, 1982.

Hancock, Les, and Morris Krieger. *The C Primer.* New York: McGraw-Hill, 1982.

Kernighan, Brian W., and P. J. Plauger. *The Elements of Programming Style.* New York: McGraw-Hill, 1978.

_____. *Software Tools in Pascal.* Reading, Mass.: Addison-Wesley, Company, 1981.

Kernighan, Brian W., and Dennis M. Ritchie. *The C Programming Language.* Englewood Cliffs, N.J.: Prentice-Hall, 1978.

Kochan, Stephen G. *Programming in C.* Rochelle Park, N.J.: Hayden Book Company, 1984.

Plum, Thomas. *Learning to Program in C.* Cardiff, N.J.: Plum-Hall, 1983.

Purdum, Jack J. *C Programming Guide.* Indianapolis, Ind.: Que Corporation, 1983.

Purdum, Jack J, Timothy C. Leslie, and Alan L. Stegemoller. *C Programmer's Library.* Indianapolis, Ind.: Que Corporation, 1984.

Users' Groups

C Users' Group
Box 97
McPherson, KS 67460

C/PM Users' Group
1651 Third Avenue
New York, NY 11028

Preface

A book can begin in several ways, but most books start with a preface like this one. It's a place for the author to adopt a friendly style to explain the purpose of the book, identify its audience, and extend thanks to those who have contributed to the project.

This book is intended to serve as one in a series of Que titles on C. Users who will gain the most from *Common C Functions* are those who already have a computer, a C compiler, and some experience in writing programs. Although I don't assume readers to be rank amateurs, I'm not trying to impress anyone either. Your curiosity about C, which may have prompted you to buy a compiler, is qualification enough.

The language has already been endorsed by experts. C's popularity is evidenced by the variety of compilers, users' groups, texts, seminars, and countless products now being written in C. The language may not be perfect, and like all features on the computer horizon, C may be eclipsed in the future by more powerful, easy-to-use, or easy-to-learn languages. But for now, C is leading a very large pack of competitors and pulling away.

C appeared in my life about the same time that I thought I was getting good at Z80 and 8088 assembler. My particular experience was in operating systems programming for CP/M-80, CP/M-86, and MS-DOS. Such work is best done in assembler, and I can't think of a better language for this kind of performance-critical application. Occasionally, I also had to write programs that did file I/O, user I/O, and noninteger math. At those times, assembler became very tedious.

Then Leor Zolman's BDS C appeared. This precursor of today's full C implementations for personal computers immediately created a loyal following among assembler hackers like myself and BASIC programmers who were ready to work with a structured, compiled language. BDS C's $150 price tag made it easy to afford, compared to other compiler languages. Almost overnight, volumes of public domain C source code from a well-supported users' group became available.

Not long after that, articles on C started appearing in even the most nontechnical places. These articles promoted C as a general-purpose language worthy of consideration by even novice programmers who were looking for a way to make a point (forgive the play on *pointer*) with their personal micros. Immediately, a large gap developed between the training materials that were available (principally Kernighan and Ritchie's *The C Programming Language*) and the growing needs of both novice and experienced programmers. And in typical fashion America's publishers began to respond.

I learned to write assembler by studying the source code contributions of unselfish (and occasionally quite talented) authors to the CP/M Users' Group. While studying this code (written in assembler), I learned some good and bad habits, and some interesting and forgettable techniques. But most of all, I learned what worked and what didn't. There is probably no more effective way to learn a language, in my opinion, than by looking at some working code, along with a reference text to discover how the author used the language to communicate to the computer what he wanted to do. I learned C the same way.

One essential quality of C separates it from PASCAL and makes C akin to assembler: the practicality of separately compiled libraries. A library is a place where you put functions (black boxes) extracted from other programs that have been generalized, tested, and saved, until a time when the functions may be required apart from the program for which they were originally designed. After Chris DeVoney encouraged me to pursue this project, I noticed that the shelves of my favorite computer bookstore were filled with half a dozen books on BASIC subroutines, and I asked, "Why not C?" C is a much better language in which to write general-purpose functions because they can be combined in libraries and recalled like "tools" to perform necessary work when they are needed. No retyping, rethinking, or recompiling is required. These libraries are commonly referred to as software tool chests!

Here, then, are my contributions to the not-so-experienced C hacker: my summary of the C language, discussed in a way that will help you learn C by examining source code and some common conversions, functions, and small programs. I hope this book will give you a head start on a robust C tool chest of your own.

Any programmer owes much to his better-trained and patient friends (confessors), and I owe a lot to many people for years of tireless help and understanding. Tim Leslie, the principal author of Ecosoft's C Compiler, is a close friend and deserves both my highest respect for competence in his art and my appreciation for many of the ideas and refinements that made their way into this book. Dr. Jack Purdum, Allen Stegemoller, and Bill Burton, who are also friends, made suggestions and criticisms that provided the polish on what at times began to look a little tarnished and scuffed up.

For the opportunity to endure the pains and pleasures of becoming a published author, I would also like to thank Chris DeVoney and the staff at Que, particularly Ginny Noble.

Steve Browning and Dr. Mitch Bodanowicz unselfishly applied their valuable time to the improvement of early drafts. I'd also like to give credit to Dr. Dave Thomas of Carleton University in Ottawa, Canada, for the concept of structures being arrays for adults. Finally, thanks are due to DY-4 Systems in Ottawa for providing me with an opportunity to learn C.

For increased legibility, the functions, programs, examples, C keywords, and file names are set in a font called Digital. This font is reproduced below.

```
ABCDEFGHIJKLMNOPQRSTUVWXYZ
abcdefghijklmnopqrstuvwxyz
0123456789
!@#$%^&*()_+~|
-=`\[]:;'<>",.?/{}
```

A ruler line is also provided to help you count the spaces in a program line.

```
        0    1    1    2    2    3    3    4    4    5    5    6
12345678901234567890123456789012345678901234567890123456789012345678901234567890
```

In program lines, square brackets ([ ]) are used to enclose an optional item, and a vertical rule (|) separates optional items that may be alternately selected.

Part I
Is This Any Way to Learn
a Programming Language?

As a believer in learning by doing, I am convinced that the approach used in this book is the best way to learn the C programming language. This view is based on my own experience and that of many self-taught friends. We learned by tirelessly examining all the source code we could find. Luckily, most of it was available in the public domain. With practice, we were able to make sense of C and gain insights about (and an affection for) the means by which data and algorithms are merged to accomplish the intent of the programmer.

The best thing that can happen to you as a beginner in C (or in any language) is to have a pile of source code dumped on you and to be told to fix it, modify it, or document it! Like most people, you probably share a disaffection for reinventing the wheel and thus would rather discover code than create it. You will have the opportunity to discover many useful C programming techniques in the functions in Part III of this book.

The purpose of Parts I and II, then, is to help you understand what's going on "behind the scenes" in the source code you'll be examining later in the functions. After reading Part II, you will know what's possible, what works, and how to do things by yourself. And your continuing education will be surprisingly affordable. You can readily find source, ranging from C compilers to ticktacktoe, in the public domain.[1]

---

[1]Steve Browning, a respected contributor to the C Users' Group, warns that not all C programs in the public domain offer compatible or worthwhile examples to study. Indeed, such programs may only suit the self-confident programmer who already understands the basics of flow control, functions, variables, compiling, linking, and I/O. A glossary of terms with which you should be familiar is included in Appendix A.

Fundamental C concepts are simple. They can be explained and understood quickly. Only through studying examples using these concepts can the subtlety of their applications be fully appreciated. If you learn well the material included in these chapters and apply what you learn to the functions in Part III, the beauty of C will unfold—and infect you, too.

So let's get started.

0

Big Pieces of the Puzzle

Files and Functions

A feature of C that may make the newcomer uneasy, but which actually is a great advantage, is C's ability to break a program into several pieces, or *files*. Furthermore, the source code to some of these pieces may not be available for your scrutiny. Having your program in pieces can be a bit disconcerting. There is a certain consolation in knowing that the listing you're holding is the sum total of the program. Actually, most programs rely on some external facilities to accomplish at least the lowest level of communication with the outside world. (These facilities include character- and block-oriented I/O, such as terminals and disk drives, which are the responsibility of the operating system—for example, CP/M, MS-DOS, or UNIX.)

Being freed from the programming overhead required to perform such low-level tasks is a great relief. You, as well as the program you're working on, can concentrate on the job at hand, leaving the details to a "black box" provided for you. In C, the concept of allowing black boxes to perform certain tasks is developed in a very elegant way, to divide large and complex programs into more comprehensible pieces. The common metaphor is a toolbox outfitted with several tools—software tools.

Files and *functions* (the building blocks of C) are the largest and most obvious pieces of a C program. Analyzing them will help you discover what the relationships are among the various tasks and how the author has divided the work. The interrelationships of files and functions in C can be very neat and orderly. Work done in either files or functions can be separated from and designed independently of the rest of the program. Larger C programs are made up of several *modules,* themselves consisting of individual functions. Each function is created to perform a small, reusable part of a larger job for which many functions are combined into a program. Designing big programs becomes an exercise in combining manageable pieces. Figure 0.1 shows how a medium-sized C program might be organized.

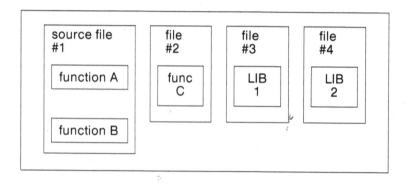

Fig. 0.1. A C program.

Both functions A and B are located in source file #1 and form a module that accomplishes the major purpose of the program. Function C is alone in source file #2 and performs some common task that is needed by many programs. These three functions represent the total source code available for this program; they are all that the programmer was obliged to write. During testing and debugging, one or both of the source code files will need to be edited and recompiled.

All C programs begin execution with a function called main. From there, control may flow to the other functions. A function can even pass control to itself recursively! Usually, control is returned to main just before the program ends.

The libraries located in files #3 and #4 represent a user library and the *standard library*[2], both with collections of frequently used functions that have previously been compiled and stored in a reduced

---

[2]Most I/O routines required for a typical program are supplied in a standard library included with most C compilers. This library provides I/O and other utility functions for a particular operating system environment. The term *standard library* is a representative but not exact description because compilers from different suppliers and for different machines sometimes have incompatible libraries.

form known as *relocatable object code*. C is quite dependent on these libraries, in part because it has no PRINT, WRITE, or READ intrinsics (that is, I/O commands) as other languages have. C programs invoke functions to perform these tasks. The functions located in the libraries have been tested and are known to work. As you can imagine, much time will be saved by not having to edit and recompile the library part of the program every time a bug is found in the new code.

To enhance the modularity of the program, you can assign different levels of privacy to the variables used by and shared among the functions. Variables used in function A can be kept private from function B. Variables available to both functions A and B may be kept private from function C, and vice versa. As in most languages, in C, some variables may be shared by all functions across the entire program. And you can even create functions that may be used only by other functions within their source module.

In summary, source files, which are collections of related functions, are called modules. The way a programmer constructs these modules indicates how functions work together to accomplish a part of the overall program. Modules also reveal which variables are used for local or temporary purposes and which variables may be used by all functions throughout the program.

As already indicated, functions are the building blocks of a C program. Within functions exist all the "action statements" that accomplish the purpose of the program. A function may act on variables passed to it, on variables that are shared by it with other functions in the module, or on variables "known" throughout the entire program. A function may create new, private variables strictly for its internal use, which are forgotten when the function ends or remembered until it is executed again. Although functions may appear to be similar to subroutines (as in FORTRAN or BASIC), functions are different in the following ways:

1. You don't "call" a function; you "invoke" it.

2. Variables passed to a function are only copies; if these variables are changed, the original ones are unaffected.

3. A function may return nothing or a single value that effectively replaces the function in the invoking program.[3]

---

[3]Don't be concerned about this apparent limitation. As you will soon discover, a function can return a small piece of information that "points" to a much larger package of data.

4. Variables created inside a function are private to the function.

5. Variables created inside a function may be transient or permanent; that is, they may have values that are garbage on entry and forgotten on exit, or be given values that are remembered through repeated invocations.

A function is merely a black box that performs some task for an invoking function. By letting the "child" function take on part of the work required by its "parent" function, the parent can keep its attention centered on completing the larger job and not on the details. This division of labor between parent and child encourages the development of many small software tools that have general application to a variety of problems. These tools can be developed, tested, and debugged independently of a particular application and stored for later use in a library.

Variables passed to a child function by the parent function are actually copies of the variables used in the parent. Thus, the original variables from the parent are protected from what goes on in the child. (Prudent, don't you think?) In fact, the exchange of information between parent and child functions is limited to the following ways that functions communicate:

1. Copies of variables are passed as parameters by the parent function to the child.

2. A single value may be returned from the child function to the parent.

3. Common variables are available to be shared among functions in the module and/or program.

A parent function can invoke a child function without any parameters or with several parameters of different types. (Another meaning for *type* will be provided later.) The "something" that a child function returns can be a value or a completion status, or nothing at all. An important note to remember is that the child function must correctly interpret the parameters passed to it from the parent function, just as the parent must be prepared to interpret what it gets back from the child. A lack of communication on the part of either parent or child function often leads to family arguments—and program failures!

Variables used within the child function, in addition to the parameters passed to it from the parent, may be completely private from any other function (usable only inside the child) or private to the module (usable only by other functions in the same source file). These variables may be created anew with each function invocation or may take their place in the computer's memory. The variables may contain garbage on entry and evaporate when control passes back to the parent, or they may be created with values that are retained between invocations.

You may not yet totally appreciate the uses to which these seemingly obscure C features (source files, modules, functions, and privacy of variables) may be put. But your understanding of C will grow as you read on.

Our perspective until now has been the "large view" of a C program. We've examined source files, modules, and functions; and we've considered, in abstract terms, how variables may or may not be shared among files and functions, and why. You have learned that some variables come and go with each invocation of a function, whereas others take up permanent residence in memory. This large view of a C program is vital to understanding the framework within which variables and constants are manipulated.

Variables and Constants

Variables and *constants* are key pieces of the C puzzle. They get declared, defined, moved, combined, organized, input, and output to accomplish the purpose of a program. To understand what happens to these data elements in a C program is to understand the program.

The popular "top down" programming technique that postpones considering the details of a program until after the "big picture" has been sketched out is perfectly compatible with C. The program can be broken down into its component functions, and some of them can be combined into modules. Variables that are required over the entire program can be given a global scope, and those required only within modules or functions can be created appropriately. A temporary variable, needed only for the purposes of an immediate function, can be used with the confidence that such a variable will do its part and then be forgotten so far as the rest of the program is concerned.

The organization of this book is likewise from the top down. Details regarding the smaller pieces of the C puzzle (variables and constants) have been put at the end of this chapter so that these details won't camouflage the beauty of the "big picture." Now that you understand what can be done with data in a C program, let's find out how to do it.

Declarations

The practical matter of identifying a variable to the C compiler is done through the variable's *declaration*. A declaration for every variable is necessary in each module in which a variable is used and is required before the variable is used. A variable used inside a function block must be declared before the action statements in the block. (A *function block* describes the group of C statements that are part of a function. The concept of a block will be given closer consideration in the section on *scope*.)

In a variable's declaration, the C compiler wants to know the following:

1. Name or identifier (Who the variable is)

2. Scope (Where it can be used)

3. Storage class (Where it is stored)

4. Type (What it can hold)

5. Scale (How much memory it takes up)

6. Initialized value (What it contains)

You will shortly discover that a subtle but important difference exists between telling the C compiler about a variable and creating one. For now, remember that the declaration of a variable is intended to let the compiler know how to create machine instructions to access the variable. After all, manipulating variables is the major work most programs do. Defining a variable, on the other hand, goes further by actually causing storage to be allocated and an initial value to be given. (As you shall see, some initial values are automatically supplied, whereas others are a product of the "leftover" contents of memory when space was reserved.)

A declaration is necessary to give information to the compiler about the variable's intended use in the program.[4] The declaration also provides some error checking so that the compiler can detect inconsistent or illogical uses of variables. A major portion of any

---

[4]Even though constants are not declared per se, they obtain default attributes, which will be discussed in Chapter 1.

source file is devoted to declaring every variable that will be used. Because many details are involved in declaring a variable, understanding data declarations must precede understanding how data is handled by C programs. This key concept (the declaration) is therefore an ideal starting place for figuring out what a C program is all about.

Identifiers

The most obvious attribute of a variable in C is its name, or *identifier*. Identifiers may be any length, but usually only the first six to eight characters are significant. Identifiers may be formed from any combination of legal characters, provided the first character is not a digit. Uppercase and lowercase letters are distinguishable by most compilers. C programs are usually written in lowercase, with the exception of any constants or keywords to which the programmer wants to bring attention. The following legal characters are permitted in a C identifier:

```
a-z
A-Z
0-9
_ (underscore)
```

A common programming practice is to give a variable a name that provides a clue to the variable's use in the program. In C, this practice is easy because identifiers can be fairly long. The use of the underscore character even allows for multiple-word identifiers. Consider the form

```
words_in_file
```

which is a single identifier used to name a variable that stores the number of words in a file. (See how easy this is!)

Scope

Where and how a variable is declared have much to do with whether it will be global or private. In C, a variable's *scope* determines in what parts of the program the variable may be referenced or "known." Its scope may extend to all parts of the program or be limited to the function or module in which the variable is declared.

The ability to keep variables private from each other on both function and module levels is a powerful tool, although it can be confusing for the beginner. This ability was included in C so that functions could be designed with the certainty that variables used inside the functions will not affect variables used outside. The "information exchange" capabilities of functions can be limited to the variables that get passed as parameters and to the variable that gets returned as a result. The essence of a software tool (and modular programming) is that what happens inside a function should be independent of what happens outside the function. A function should also perform predictably (to the extent possible) with a variety of input.

Variables declared outside functions have a broader scope than variables declared inside functions. This arrangement is logical because variables declared within a function should be there only for the internal use of the function. These variables are not "visible" outside the function. Even variables of the same name declared within different functions or modules are kept distinct by the compiler (with the most local variable taking precedence). Variables declared outside functions, however, have a broader scope, at least broad enough to be used by the functions found in the same source file, and possibly broad enough to be used by any function in other modules as well.

The C compiler knows what scope to assign a variable from the location of the variable's declaration: inside or outside a block. A block is the group of action statements making up a function. (Statements will be discussed in Chapter 3.) Fundamentally, a block is defined by a matched set of *braces,* as indicated in figure 0.2.

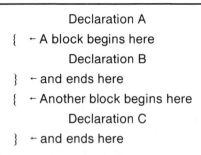

Declaration A
{ ← A block begins here
Declaration B
} ← and ends here
{ ← Another block begins here
Declaration C
} ← and ends here

Fig. 0.2. C blocks.

A variable declared inside a block (as in declarations for variables B and C in fig. 0.2) can be used only within that block. The scope of a variable declared outside a block, as in declaration A, *may* be as broad as the entire program, but the variable can *always* be used by the functions within its source file. The keyword static may be included in the variable's declaration to protect the variable from functions outside the variable's module.

For every block that is created, a new scope level is obtained. Functions, in particular, define a block by having their openings and closings marked with braces. But even within functions, blocks of a subordinate scope can be created if needed. (And such blocks are commonly created, as we shall see in subsequent chapters.)

The static scope may also apply to a function. If a function is declared by using this keyword, the function may be invoked only by other functions in the same module.

Storage Class

Where a variable is stored and whether its storage space is transient or permanent are determined by the variable's *storage class*. This feature of a variable dictates whether its storage is allocated in main memory by the compiler at compile time or "on the stack" as temporary storage, existing only so long as a function is executing. This distinction may be new to programmers who think that variables, once created, go on "living" forever.

One advantage of a variable that is created temporarily is that it requires storage space only when it is "alive." Since this type of variable is located dynamically (at run time) on the local stack of the function, the function can be invoked *recursively,* without intermediate results being lost. This important programming technique makes the solution of some problems easier and more efficient.

As in the case of a variable's scope, a variable's storage class is communicated to the compiler in two combined ways: from the location of the variable's declaration and from the keywords associated with the variable.

All variables declared within a function block are assumed to be of the auto class. (A similar class, register, will be discussed later.) The auto class is the most transient type, with storage for variables being allocated and deallocated automatically every time the function is entered and exited. Although the keyword auto is available, it is very seldom used because auto is the default class.

Adding somewhat to the confusion for which C is criticized, the keyword static also plays a role in storage class determination. If the declaration for a variable within a function block includes the keyword static, the variable's storage space is permanently allocated by the compiler (at compile time), and the variable's value is initialized to zero before the program begins. Unlike an auto, with storage space created "on the fly" and a value that is garbage on entry and lost on completion, a static retains its value between function invocations.

Declaring a variable outside a function block tells the compiler to do two things: make the variable permanent and initialize it to zero before the program begins. Such a variable is said to be of the external storage class. Remember that a variable with this storage class may have two different scopes. If declared with the keyword static, the variable can be used only within the immediate module; otherwise, the variable is global, that is, visible throughout the entire program.

Table 0.1 organizes the scope and storage class possibilities of any variable. "Inside" and "outside" refer to whether the variable is declared inside or outside a function block.

The keyword extern has a different and practical use. When external storage class variables (those highlighted in the preceding table) are declared in a particular source file, the variable is said to be *defined;* that is, space in memory is reserved. The variable may also be *initialized* (given an initial value to be used at the start of the program). Functions in other source files may need to access this variable. How do you suppose the compiler finds out that the variable var1 declared in module #1 is the same var1 that is declared again in module #2? (Remember that a variable must be declared before it is used in each source file.) The answer lies in the use of the keyword extern, which must be used with all but one of the declarations for the variable in the modules in which it is used. This keyword tells the compiler that somewhere a declaration *and* definition of this variable have already been made, and thus not to provide them more than once.

Most linkers will not allow multiple definitions to pass without generating an error. Note also that if a variable's declaration is marked with extern, the variable may not be initialized. This makes sense because no space is being reserved for the variable.

The only difference between auto and register storage class variables is that the compiler attempts to place register variables in

Table 0.1

		Storage Class	
		Permanent	Transient
S c o p e	Private to a function	Inside function block; marked `static`	Inside function block; assumed to be `auto` or `register`
	Private to a module	Outside function block; marked `static`	Not allowed
	Global	Outside function block; default	Not allowed

machine registers. (Or at least the language specification says that registers are where they should be stored.) The `register` storage class allows the programmer to tell the compiler that a particular variable is needed so frequently that it should be located in one of the internal, high-speed registers of the microprocessor. This storage location is obviously transient (because the next function would likely store its own data there). (Most compilers for 8- and 16-bit machines, such as the 8080/5, Z80, and 8088/86, can't effectively accommodate the `register` storage class because of the few number of registers available.)

Data Types

Having worked our way down from source files and functions to how variables are stored and protected, let's now examine the concept of *type*. C gives the programmer only a few data types to work with but allows almost infinite variety in the combinations that are possible. Table 0.2 displays all the *simple* data types available. (*Aggregate* types, made from combinations of simple types, will be discussed later in this chapter.)

Table 0.2
Simple C Data Types

char	float
int	double
unsigned	function
long	pointer
short	

Subordinating the keywords unsigned, long, and short to int indicates that they are three additional "subtypes" of the basic type int. According to the original language specification, Kernighan and Ritchie's *The C Programming Language,* these three keywords were to be used as adjectives to modify the C compiler's interpretation of a variable that could otherwise be treated as an int. Most compilers now allow the use of the adjective alone without out the type name int.

A variable's type directly determines the amount of memory that the compiler will allocate for the variable's storage. This allocation is important because the compiler must generate the correct machine instructions when the variable is referenced. The type directly dictates the maximum and minimum value (or values, in the case of aggregate types) that can be stored in a variable. Table 0.3 lists the simple data types and indicates the typical range of values each may hold.

A declaration of a simple variable is made by using one of the keywords (in table 0.3) in front of the variable's identifier. (Function and pointer types are special cases and are treated separately in this chapter.) The area set aside for declarations is usually well marked and should include a description of the use of the variable. The general form of a declaration for a simple variable is

```
[extern] | [static] type identifier [= value];
```

We have already discussed the optional use of the keywords extern and static. (They may not be used together.) In this declaration, type is replaced by one of the types described previously (not including pointer or function). The identifier is the name by which the variable will be referenced. As in most other languages, in C, use of the name produces the value held at the memory location reserved for that name. (Later, when pointers, functions, and aggregate types are treated, this definition will be extended.) The

**Table 0.3
Values That Can Be Stored in Simple Data Types
(Typical for 8- and 16-bit Computers)**

`char`	A character in the host machine's character set or an integer n where $-128 <= n <= 127$
`int`	An integer n where $-32768 <= n <= 32767$
`unsigned int`	An integer n where $0 <= n <= 65535$
`short int`	An integer n where $-32768 <= n <= 32767$
`long int`	An integer n where $-2147483648 <= n <= 2147483647$
`unsigned long int`	An integer n where $0 <= n <= 4294967295$
`float`	A floating-point number n where $10E-39 <= n <= 10E38$ with 6 digits of accuracy
`double`	A floating-point number n where $10E-39 <= n <= 10E38$ with 14 digits of accuracy

function symbol: ( )	The value returned from a function, which may be an `int`, `long`, `double`, or pointer type
pointer	An `unsigned` integer capable of representing any memory address at which data may be stored

Differences exist among machines of varying capabilities, and the environment for which a program is written should be considered when determining what data can go into which variables. Caution should always be applied to assignments between pointers and `int`s or `long`s, however. Depending on the compiler implementation, you may be surprised and disappointed at how such conversions are made.

optional use of the = `value` part of the declaration allows a variable to be initialized with a value prior to being used in the program. (Rules for initializing all data types are located after the discussion of aggregate types.) Finally, the semicolon at the end of the declaration makes it a legal C *statement*.

The following declarations for simple variables are taken from the functions that appear in Part III:

```
unsigned int counter;    /* a typical loop counter        */
long int number;         /* a big number                  */
char n;                  /* a small number                */
char key, guess;         /* 2 variables; each can hold     */
                         /* a single ASCII character      */
float mortgage_balance;  /* a floating-point value        */
static int tolls;        /* a permanent storage class     */
                         /* int, which will retain its    */
                         /* value between function        */
                         /* invocations even if declared  */
                         /* inside a function block       */
extern double loan;      /* a floating-point number,      */
                         /* space for which was           */
                         /* allocated elsewhere with a    */
                         /* similar declaration without   */
                         /* the keyword 'extern'          */
```

Function

The function type can't hold a value per se and therefore cannot be described by the value that the function might have held. Like any variable, however, a function may be declared to tell the compiler what type of data is returned from the function, and *must* be declared if the variable returned is not an int.

A child function that returns no value to the parent is sometimes declared with the type void. Notice that void isn't mentioned in table 0.3. (void was not a part of the original language specification.) This type is cleverly self-explanatory and optional. The compiler assumes that every function returns an int unless told otherwise. The fact that the int might not be used is of no concern to the compiler. The real use of the void function type is for documentation. Declaring a function with void puts the reader on notice that no value is going to be returned. Some compilers will complain if such a function tries to pass back a value. There is even a UNIX utility, lint (used to check C syntax for portability and other problems), that will complain if a parent function attempts to use a value returned from a child function declared with void.

Functions are declared with a form almost identical to that for other simple variables:

```
[static] type identifier();
```

The `static` keyword may be used to tell the compiler that this function is invocable only by the other functions in the immediate source module. The type is replaced by one of the simple data types (or one of the *terminating* types discussed later). If the function returns a pointer, the type of data pointed to must also be declared. Notice that the symbol for function, ( ), follows the identifier and that a semicolon is tacked on the end. Because the declaration of a function cannot "reserve space" for the function, using the keyword `extern` is not necessary. Following are some examples:

```
double log();          /* declares the function: log  */
                       /* returns a double            */

int set_up();          /* tells the compiler that     */
                       /* set_up returns an int; it   */
                       /* would have been assumed     */

char *alloc();         /* declares that alloc returns */
                       /* a pointer to chars          */
```

This discussion of functions has focused on their declarations and not on how functions are created or used. Creating and using functions will be covered in Part II, What C Programs Look Like.

Pointer

The declaration of a pointer variable is similar to the declaration of a function because in both cases the compiler needs to know that the variable actually holds the address of something and what data type that "something" is (in the case of a function, its entry point address and what the function returns, respectively). The general form of a declaration for a pointer is

```
[extern] | [static] type *identifier [= value];
```

As with other simple types, the pointer type may be declared with the keywords `extern` or `static`. The pointer type also may be initialized. But the real difference lies in the use of the pointer symbol *, which is placed in front of the identifier. This symbol tells the compiler that the value of the variable is actually the address of a data item of the type declared. The address can be that of just about anything. And the use of pointers to everything—such as to simple or aggregate data types, to functions, and to other pointers—can be justified, given the right underlying data structure or application. Regardless of what a pointer points to, however, the pointer is always the same size: big enough to hold the address of any place in memory.

Pointers get a lot of attention in C because they provide a very simple and powerful way of accessing data: through a variable. Think of a pointer as a telescope through which an observer may peer into a data world comprised of the types of data that the pointer has been declared to oversee. The program is the observer, and the variable may be "aimed at" (given the address of) any particular item of data. Beginning programmers are sometimes discouraged by the results of their first attempts to use pointers. Many flawed programs result from the following improper use of pointers:

1. The pointer may not be aimed at anything. This likely results in the program's looking at garbage (usually a result of declaring a pointer variable and never giving it a value, that is, the address of anything).

2. The pointer may be given a value of zero, which is, by agreement, an invalid place to point (the default value for variables, including pointers, of the external storage class).

3. The pointer may be looking at data of a type that is different from that which the pointer is expecting to see. If so, the program may misinterpret the data.

Programmers use pointers because they can manipulate very complex or large data structures through a single, small variable. C obliges (or more correctly, compels) the programmer to know where certain variables are stored. Knowing what is there (by the declaration) and where to find it (through the pointer) can offer a more efficient means of manipulating data than handling the variable itself. Pointers are used frequently in C. Accessing a variable through its address is known as *indirection*.

When data needs to be shared between functions, one method is to pass as a parameter a pointer to the data. As previously indicated, a child function only receives a copy of the variable passed to the child by the parent; the original variable in the parent can't be changed. But if the parent passes the child a pointer to the variable, the child may have the same access to the original variable as did the parent.

When several of a particular kind of data item are arranged in memory, access to any one item can be made by simply adjusting where the pointer points. This adjustment hinges on the concept of *scale* (the size of the memory location occupied by the variable), which will be discussed shortly.

A particularly common data type for which C uses pointers is the *character string*. You will recall that a character string is a sequence of (usually) printable (ASCII) characters that a programmer might use to print a message on the terminal, to put words in a file, or to send as a command to a function. C treats these strings in the following special ways:

1. Handled exclusively through pointers

2. Null terminated (that is, the strings end with a Ø)

When a programmer constructs such strings in memory, a place for the zero must always be reserved and added to the number of memory locations required to store the string. When the C compiler creates a *string constant* by finding a sequence of characters between double quotation marks (" ") in the source code, a null is appended automatically, and the variable created is a pointer to (that is, the address of) the first character of the string. Specifically, a variable is created with a value equal to the address where the string has been stored by the compiler.

In the familiar example of a programmer's first program in which the string

    "Hello, world"

is printed on the console, the C compiler actually stores the following sequence in memory:

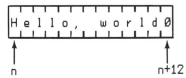

→ sequential memory locations →

The compiler might place the address of the H, represented by *n*, into a variable, here called ptr (a pointer):

```
┌───┐
│ n │   =  address of the H
└───┘
 ptr
```

---

†Don't confuse this 0 with the ASCII character 'Ø', which actually is the number 32.

The declaration of such a variable is

```
char *ptr;
```

The * marks the variable as being of type pointer, and the char sig-
nifies that the pointer will be pointing to data of that type. The identifier (name) of the variable is ptr. (The data to which ptr points has
no name, just a place in memory.) The function that prints the string
is only given the value that is in ptr, (that is, the address of the
string) to work with. Because the function knows that it will be
passed a variable which is a pointer to a string of chars, and also
that the end of the string will be marked with a null, the function
confidently prints the character at the pointer, increments the
pointer, and keeps on printing the characters until the function
finds the null.

In this declaration example, the compiler has been told only what
kind of information the variable ptr will hold. A value for ptr is not
given. Giving ptr a value is called *initialization*. Like other types, a
string pointer may be initialized quite easily during its declaration.
In this same example, if we want to declare the variable ptr and
initialize it with the address of the string "Hello, world", all we have
to do is write

```
char *ptr = "Hello, world";
```

Always remember that the double quotation marks cause a little
magic to happen: they produce a pointer to the character string
they wrap.

More complicated examples of the use of pointers are explained
in the functions in Part III. Remember that in operations using
pointers, pointers to any data type have the same features as pointers to the characters in strings. Following is a summary of char-
acteristics of pointers:

1. A pointer holds an address where data of any type (char, int,
double, aggregate types, etc.) may be found. The address value is
what you get by using the variable's name without the *.

2. The type of data pointed to must be described in the pointer's
declaration.

3. The data item found where the pointer points is accessed by
placing an asterisk (*) in front of the variable name.

4. The pointer's value must be changed before you can look at a
different data item in a sequence.

5. Declaration of a pointer variable only reserves space where an address may be stored, and space will be reserved only if the keyword extern is not used. Only an initializer can make a declaration of a pointer point anywhere.

Aggregate Types

The following aggregate data types may be formed by combining the simple types already described:

array
struct
union

Aggregate types allow the programmer to manipulate groups of data of one type or mixed types with one variable name. These groups include *arrays* and *structures*, respectively. Another aggregate type, union, gives the programmer the ability to store different types at the same location in memory. Thus, the same variable (memory space) can be interpreted in different ways by the compiler. Since most programs deal with data in groups, these C data types should become quite familiar to you.

Arrays

Arrays are common in programming parlance: they define a set of data, all of the same type, that is stored sequentially in memory so that any one item may be accessed by knowing the address of the base of the array and adding the product of the item number wanted times its size. This location algorithm is never actually performed by the programmer; the compiler does all the dirty work. The compiler knows how much memory each item of an array requires and remembers that quantity for such calculations. (The size, or scale, of a data type is fully discussed later in this chapter.)

Arrays of multiple dimensions provide a way to store information in subgroups so that a whole can be divided into many parts, each of which may be further divided into smaller parts. This division can even be taken beyond the two- or three-dimensional organizations that have physical representations.

Data in an array is accessed by means of an *index*. This index is nothing more than the item number already mentioned. Usually, the compiler locates the array in memory at compile time. Unlike a pointer, an array does not have a variable to store the address of the start of an array. In the program the base address of an array is a constant. The address never gets changed; an offset equal to the product of the data type's scale times the index is added to the base address to locate the item wanted.

In a more complex, multiply dimensioned array, indexes are more like ZIP codes: each digit (a dimension), starting on the left, gets you into regions (subgroups) closer to the part of the country (data) in which you're interested. If you stop supplying indexes before you get to the last dimension, you may be left stranded in a very big region. In that case, C leaves you with the address of the start of the region. All along the way, C performs the calculations to get you from the base of the array to the piece of data (or region) you want.

Arrays are declared by using square brackets ([ ]). In C, a pair of them is appended to the variable name, when it is declared, for every dimension needed. (This method is different from that of other languages which use a single pair of parentheses or square brackets, with integers separated by commas for each dimension required.) An item is extracted from the array by supplying integer values (the indexes) between the brackets. The standard form for the declaration of an array type is

```
[extern] | [static] type identifier[size] [= { data }];
```

The optional extern or static keywords used before have the same meaning here. The type tells the C compiler what type of data items makes up the array. The identifier tells the compiler what the array will be called. And the opening and closing square brackets after the identifier tell the compiler that this data will be ordered contiguously in memory and accessed by indexes. The size must be given if we want to allocate space for the array. If the size is omitted, the compiler will assume that the declaration is for information only, that is, to indicate that the identifier is an array of types.

If a multiply dimensioned array were needed instead, additional sets of brackets and sizes would be added after those shown. The total number of items in an array is always the product of the sizes.

The identifier, if used later in the program without the brackets, will produce the address of the beginning of the array. This use of the identifier is like a pointer because a pointer's identifier without the preceding asterisk produces the pointer's value, that is, the address of some data item. However, no variable in memory stores an array's address. An array base address, then, can't be changed during the program's execution the way a pointer value can. The only thing that can be done with the value represented by an array identifier is to add an offset to its value either to find a particular element by providing a fully qualified index, or to find the address of a subgroup by omitting one or more trailing index levels.

The size in the form above is replaced by an integer that instructs the compiler to allocate enough memory to store the number of data types indicated. If the array being declared is of the external storage class, that is, declared outside a function block, the array will be zeroed before the program is started. Otherwise, if the array is declared inside a function block, the array's contents will be garbage. (Note: The amount of memory reserved will be equal to the number of items times the size of each item. Again, the concept of scale becomes important.)

The optional = { data } indicates how arrays (and other aggregate data types to be discussed shortly) may be initialized. The opening brace marks the beginning of a series of comma-separated data items that will be used to initialize sequential locations in the array. The closing brace ends the series and is followed by a semicolon. The declaration

```
int colors[] = {0, 1, 2, 3};
```

is equivalent to

```
int colors[4];

colors[0]=0;
colors[1]=1;
colors[2]=2;
colors[3]=3;
```

In the first declaration, the C compiler was left to figure out how many items were in the array and thus how much memory to reserve. (Notice that no number appears in the brackets.) These locations were then initialized with the values shown in braces. In the equivalent form that follows, the declaration is made for a variable, colors, which will be used to reference four ints. Then the members of the array are given values.

The variable colors can be declared to be of type array, without space being reserved or initialized for the element, if the following is written:

```
extern colors[];
```

This form lets the compiler know that colors is an array of ints and can be accessed as such if necessary. This use is common for the declaration used inside a function of an array variable passed as a parameter. Another example occurs when a second module needs access to the array colors. You've already seen that variables need to be declared before use in each module in which they appear, with the "space reserving" declaration (definition) being made in only one module. (Where the declaration would be preceded by the key word extern.)

The first element of an array is item number 0, which is accessed by placing a zero between the brackets. The array starts at the memory address occupied by this element. The last item of an array n items long is item n-1. Remember that the number of items is used to make space when an array is declared, but when the array is accessed, the item number is used.

Items in an array don't necessarily have to be one of the simple types. The items can themselves be aggregates, as long as the entire aggregate is repeated for each item. Multiply dimensioned arrays are really just arrays of arrays. (You'll soon see how arrays of more complicated structures can be extremely useful.)

Data organized in arrays may also be accessed through the use of pointers. In fact, the C compiler treats arrays and pointers alike internally. The real difference is that the array's base address is not stored as a variable in memory the way a pointer value is. During compilation, the compiler locates the array in memory and remembers its address and the scale of the array's members when the compiler creates the machine instructions to access them. In the declaration

```
char message[13];
```

in which each item is given the following appropriate value

```
message[0] = 'H';    message[5] = ',';  message[10] = 'l';
message[1] = 'e';    message[6] = ' ';  message[11] = 'd';
message[2] = 'l';    message[7] = 'w';  message[12] = '\0';
message[3] = 'l';    message[8] = 'o';
message[4] = 'o';    message[9] = 'r';
```

passing the name of the array message to the printing function used in the earlier example would produce the exact same results: "Hello, world".

Arrays are preferable to pointers when access to a sequence of data items must be random, that is, when there is no way to predict which item will be needed next. A text string is accessed starting at the beginning and continuing on through the end. Such a string is well served by a pointer because access is usually made sequentially from low to high memory addresses. For a pointer to access data randomly, the pointer's value must be changed to point to some new place; this change may produce the side effect of losing track of the base address. And the base address may be required later on in the program! If the base address is important for later accesses or if access to a data structure is random, then an array is the better choice.

A good example of a multiply dimensioned array is one that may be used to store the frequency of cards appearing during a card game. Such an array may be declared as

```
int cards[4][14];
```

which tells the compiler that space must be reserved to fit 4 * 14 = 56 ints in memory. But there are 52 cards, you say? Alas, the real world has chosen not to play with the zero of spades, so the 0 of each suit in our array is wasted. It is far easier to conform our data structure to the real world than to do the reverse. Providing an unused element here allows us to use the card and suit values directly as indexes and to avoid any adjustments.

The array is divided into 4 subgroups whose suits are numbered 0, 1, 2, and 3 for spades, diamonds, clubs, and hearts, respectively. Each group contains 14 cards: eleven are numbered 0, 1 (ace), 2, 3, and so on; three include the face cards J-11, Q-12, and K-13. The number of times a card has been dealt can be obtained simply by using the suit and the card number as indexes. For example, to get the number of aces dealt, just sum

```
  cards[0][1]
+ cards[1][1]
+ cards[2][1]
+ cards[3][1]
-----------------------------
  total aces
```

The following form tells you how many hearts have been dealt:

```
  cards[3][1]
+ cards[3][2]
+ cards[3][3]
+ cards[3][4]
+ cards[3][5]
+ cards[3][6]
+ cards[3][7]
+ cards[3][8]
+ cards[3][9]
+ cards[3][10]
+ cards[3][11]
+ cards[3][12]
+ cards[3][13]
---------------------------------
  total hearts
```

Finally, the form

```
cards[1][5]
```

tells you how many times you saw the five of diamonds.

The compiler can also provide you with information about the address of each subgroup. If you use the form

```
cards[1]
```

somewhere in a program, you will get the starting address of the series of 14 elements that stores the number of diamonds dealt. This value is computed at compile time and is not stored as a variable anywhere, but is a constant.

You can't use arrays for organizations of data of mixed types. C provides such a capability with structures.

Structures

Structures are "arrays for adults" because the regular organization of identical data types allowed in an array is upgraded to allow any arbitrary combination of different data types. Whereas the elements of an array are accessed by indexes, structure elements have *member names*. Structures make working with "packages" of data simpler and more comprehensible because the whole package can be referenced through a single variable name: the structure's identifier. Structures are recommended when several related variables must be manipulated together, especially in cases where multiple packages with the same organization are required (an array of structures).

As with any other variable, a structure must be declared. A structure declaration has many components, some of which will be familiar, and some of which may not. The general form of a structure is

```
[extern] | [static] struct [tag] {
                              declaration
                              declaration
                              declaration

                              } [identifier][= { data }];
```

Once again, the declaration may include the keywords `extern` or `static` to indicate the variable's storage class and/or scope. Type is not present because a structure is a repository for different types (and is itself a *terminating* type). The keyword `struct` informs the compiler that the organization of data types following the structure is to be regarded as an indivisible data package. The optional *tag* provides a shorthand way to tell the compiler about subsequent uses of the same organization of data.

The optional identifier (this is the first time that a name of a variable has been optional) points out the two uses of this form. When the identifier is omitted, the declaration just tells the compiler about an organization of data items (its members) that has been given a tag, or shorthand name. But using the identifier, with or without a tag, goes beyond simply describing what the structure looks like and causes the compiler to reserve space in memory for the variable. The variable so created is named by the identifier. Like other variables (and aggregates, in particular), the identifier may be initialized by using a sequence of comma-delimited values bound on either side by opening and closing braces and concluded with a semicolon.

The purpose of the tag is convenience. When other variables having the identical organization are used, a description of the structure's contents may be omitted, and the tag may be used in place of the description.

Each of the structure's members is itself a data declaration, incorporating a type and an identifier, which becomes the member name. Both simple and aggregate types are allowed. A member of a structure can be a structure, an array, a union (to be discussed shortly), or even another structure similar to the one in which the member is being defined! Sufficient space is reserved in memory to hold these members, and the compiler keeps track of the location (offset) in the structure at which each member can be found.

To access the value held by a member, use the form

```
identifier. member
```

in which the identifier is the name given to the structure, and the member is the name of the data item to access. The following examples should help to clarify how this accessing is done.

A structure that sets aside an area of memory big enough to hold three ints is

```
struct {
      int member1;
      int member2;
      int member3;
} name;
```

in which the notation int memberx is simply a declaration of a member whose type is int. The structure doesn't have a tag. The structure does have a place reserved in memory, however, where the member variables may be stored. This reserved space is a consequence of adding the identifier after the closing brace (although defining the structure doesn't make it contain anything useful yet). The variable name is given the type struct. A programmer would access member1 by using

```
name. member1
```

The general form is

```
identifier. member
```

This technique of creating a structure is limited to a single occurrence because only the variable has been given a name; the structure's organization has not. In practice, it is often more useful to give a structure a tag so that multiple occurrences of the same data structure can be referenced more easily. Consider the example

```
struct group {
      int number;
      double average_age;
      char *leader;
};
```

in which `group` is the structure's tag. Because this form has no identifier following the closing brace, no space is reserved in memory. The compiler is simply being told that such an organization exists. Later, a place in memory can be created and given a name (defined) with the general form

```
struct tag identifier;
```

The example

```
struct group children;
```

tells the compiler to create a variable `children` of type `struct` in memory, with an organization of data items described by the tag `group`. You can imagine that there will be other variables, such as

```
struct group adults;
struct group seniors;
struct group teens;
```

The advantage of using a tag is that the compiler needs to be told only once about the organization of data types that constitute a structure which may be shared by many variables. The declaration of a structure using only the tag reserves no memory and doesn't create a variable.

Finally, these two ways of declaring a structure may be combined so that the structure is tagged and a variable is created with space reserved in memory, as in the form

```
struct cars {
     unsigned int units;
     float price;
     char *model;
} olds, ford, chevy;
```

which creates three variables all at once.

If you need to use members of a structure in two different source files, you have the obligation to declare the structure in both places. But in only one place can the structure be defined by adding an identifier, as indicated in table 0.4.

Sometimes structures are needed as members of other structures. If this statement sounds a little confusing, a simple illustration will show you how natural this data organization can be. Suppose you run across a program that manages the affairs of a bowling league. You may be faced with the following declarations:

```
struct bowler {          /* statistics for a single */
     int high_series;     /* bowler                  */
     int high_game;
     float average;
     char *name;
};

struct league {               /* information about */
     char *sponsor;            /* each team         */
     int games_played;
     struct bowler member[4];  /* four team members */
} team[32];                    /* 32 teams          */
```

Somewhere in the program you may find

```
team[3].member[0].name    /* to access a        */
                          /* pointer to the     */
                          /* name of the first  */
                          /* member of the 4th  */
                          /* team (the leader)  */
```

which is used to print the player's name.

C is quite capable of performing this multiple-level data "search" and is very efficient at it. By choosing identifiers that convey some thought about what the complex constructions are trying to do, the code is easier to understand and maintain by someone other than its original author.

Table 0.4

In source file #1:	In source file #2:
```struct tag { int member1; char *member2; }; struct tag variable;```	```struct tag { int member1; char *member2; }; extern struct tag variable;```

Another way to access members of a structure is to use a pointer. As previously mentioned, pointers are big business in C. And pointers to structures are in big demand. A pointer to a structure passed as a parameter is the only way to give the child function access to all the structure's members if the scope of the structure is not the same as, or higher than, the invoked function.[5] (In other words, the structure is of the external storage class, or marked `static` and used by functions within the structure's module.)

The general form for declaring a pointer to a structure is

```
struct tag {
     member1;
     member2;
     member3;
} *identifier;
```

or

```
struct tag *identifier;
```

in which `*identifier` no longer defines a place in memory big enough to hold the member variables. Here the identifier only defines a variable that will hold the address at which data organized as shown can be found. The use made of this variable is identical to that of other pointers: the variable can be used to retrieve *indirectly* the data to which the variable points by using the form

```
identifier->member
```

Notice the use of -> in place of the period (.) used previously. This convenient replacement is allowed by the designers of the language to avoid an otherwise awkward form. Again, our purpose is to retrieve the data to which the pointer points. This pointer is no different from any pointer—right? Well, almost no different. The astute reader will remember that to retrieve the variable to which a pointer points, we used an asterisk (*). So why not use one here? The answer has to do with the "binding" of the . and * operators: the . binds tighter.

The less concise but equivalent form is

```
(*identifier).member
```

which tells us to get the value pointed to by the identifier, offset by the location of the member within the structure. The asterisk lets the compiler know that we want the contents of the variable's iden-

---

[5]The most recent description of the C language allows the passing of entire structures as parameters to functions, the assignment of structures, and the returning of structures from functions. These features were not in the original language specification. You should check your compiler documentation for use of these features.

tifier, which is an address. The parentheses tell the compiler to get that address first. And the period says to add the offset where we can find the member. This form is harder to write and was therefore contracted to the shorthand -> as a convenience.

The answer to the previous question about the pointer was "almost" because there is really no way to get any data from the use of *identifier alone. You may have assumed that there is a way, but this assumption is based on an incomplete understanding of how pointers work. For example, if we wanted to work with the int pointed to when we declared the pointer

```
int *number;
```

we would use *number. But since the type of identifier in the earlier example was struct, then *identifier is invalid without the period attached. *identifier won't, for example, get you the first data item in the structure.[6] The compiler will complain if *identifier is used.

Unions

Unions are used less frequently than the other aggregate types but nevertheless provide a useful capability. A union defines a single place in memory where more than one data type may be stored, but only one at a time. A union allows access to variables of different types and sizes (either simple or aggregate types) at the same place in memory but at different times. In other words, a union enables you to interpret data at the same location in different ways—something C usually penalizes you for. Because unions provide a way for you to take control of how the C compiler treats data, they are used in more sophisticated applications. The programmer assumes the responsibility for using the correct access means at run time.

A union is essentially identical to a structure in the ways they are declared. Either may be given a tag, an identifier, or both at the same time. Either a union or a structure may be declared with the keywords extern or static. Unions, however, may not be initialized because interpretation of their contents comes at run time, *not* compile time.

---

[6]Again, the most recent changes that allow structures to be treated like other nonaggregate types will allow such a construction (*identifier) and will produce the entire structure, but still not the first member.

The general form for the declaration of a union is

```
[extern] | [static] union [tag] {
                        declaration
                        declaration
                        declaration
                    } [identifier ];
```

The optional tag is used to give this organization of contents a name so that it may be used in other declarations. As previously indicated, the use of the optional identifier creates a variable with space reserved in memory. For a union the space reserved is equal in size to that of the union's largest member. Member names in structures give information to the compiler about what type of data the compiler will find and where (offset from the base of the structure) the compiler can find it. The member name of a union conveys information about only what type of data the compiler can find. All data is put into the union at its base, with only one member resident at a time.

Let's look at some brief examples. The general form

```
union {
      int member1;
      long member2;
      double member3;
} a_union;
```

advises the compiler that the variable a_union, of type union, should be placed in memory with space reserved equal to the size of its largest member, a double.

Access to a member of a union is accomplished in the same way as access to a member of a structure. The general form

```
identifier. member
```

informs the running program that the variable currently occupying the union should be interpreted as the type associated with the declaration of the member. From the previous declaration, the expression

```
a_union. member1
```

instructs the running program to interpret the variable stored at a_union as if the variable were an int. Similarly, the form

```
union a_tag {
      int member1;
      float member2;
};
```

describes a union, with members as declared, and with the tag a_tag, which can be used elsewhere when variables are required of that combination. And the form

```
union a_tag {
      int member1;
      float member2;
} a_union;
```

does both.

The following example makes use of the features of a union to allow a program to gain access to normally indivisible parts of a pointer value, that is, the address of an object. These features are useful because any memory location within the 8088 microprocessor (the one used in the IBM PC) is actually composed of two values: a segment and an offset.[7] The segment defines in which 64K region of memory to look; the offset tells how far from the start of this region the data begins. Pointers capable of representing addresses in this system are made from two unsigned ints.

In the example, the union provides a program with the means to access either the entire pointer value, or the segment or offset parts individually. The form

```
union {
      unsigned int address[2];
      int *pointer;
} storage;
```

assumes that the type of data to which this pointer points is an int. This union allows us to reference the pointer value by the form

```
storage. pointer
```

or the offset value by

```
storage. address[0]
```

---

[7]Two int addresses are required in the 8088 microprocessor because it can access up to 1M (1 megabyte) of memory, which is outside the range of a single int. Many compilers, however, allow only a portion of memory, up to 64K, to be accessed and therefore provide only one int pointer. The former is often termed the "large" model, whereas the latter is described as a "small" model.

or the segment value by the form

```
storage.address[1]
```

In the program that uses this pointer, the int to which it points is accessed by

```
*(storage.pointer)
```

which means that the value from the union is retrieved before you use the value as an address to point to the int you want. (Because the . binds more tightly than the *, the parentheses aren't really required here.)

We can construct pointers to unions in the exact same way that pointers to structures are constructed. To continue with this example, let's place a value in the union that is a pointer to some data. First, declare a pointer to union and a pointer data item by the form

```
union {
     unsigned int address[2];
     int *pointer;
} *storage;

int *ptr;
```

Now, to fill the union with a pointer value, we have to access the union variable as if it were a pointer and then assign it a value. These steps are accomplished by the form

```
storage->pointer = ptr; †
```

which will place the address of the int pointed to by ptr (not the int itself because we omitted the asterisk) where the pointer to the union points. As before, we can retrieve the offset value of the pointer by using

```
storage->address[0]
```

or the segment value by using

```
storage->address[1]
```

Access to the data pointed to by the pointer in this union may be obtained by the form

```
*(storage->pointer)
```

---

†Beware of this construction on machines other than the 8088, 8086, or 80286.

An important detail in this example deserves more consideration. All the preceding statements are legal and will compile without error. But neither the pointer to the int nor the pointer to the union was initialized in the code that was shown. All that happened was to move the address of an int that the C compiler hadn't located yet (that is, garbage) into a place that likewise hadn't been assigned yet (in other words, into the "twilight zone").

This example should reinforce a characteristic of pointers already mentioned: when a pointer variable is declared, it does not automatically point anywhere. Enough space is reserved to hold an address that can point to anywhere in memory, but no address is put there! To work as intended, an int must be created in memory, and the variable ptr made to equal the int's address; space for the union must be allocated, and its address placed in the variable storage. Then the line

```
storage->pointer = ptr;
```

will have the desired effect and not produce an untimely system crash.

Scale

Every data type has an associated *scale,* which refers to the number of bytes the type consumes when it is placed in memory. Scale is also used by the compiler to move among data when more than one of a single type are grouped together (as with arrays and structures).

The simple data types are given sizes by the compiler's author. These sizes are based on the capabilities of the microprocessor for which the compiler was designed. (In other words, scale is an environment-dependent feature of the language.) Table 0.5 shows the sizes of the simple data types for most 8- and 16-bit microprocessor C compilers. These types may be combined into aggregate types to yield an infinite variety of sizes.

When looking at groups of data, the C compiler needs to know by what factor (scale) to increment through memory in order to find the next group. For example, when an array of floats is arranged in memory, a float occurs every four bytes. When an array of chars is declared, a char is found at each byte. An array of ints has an int at every other byte. The compiler will automatically add eight to the address held in a pointer variable that accesses doubles

Table 0.5
Typical C Data Sizes in Bytes (Indicating Scale)
8- and 16-Bit CPUs

char	1
short	2
int	2
long	4
float	4
double	8

pointer
    8088 large
    model
	2
	
	4

each time the pointer is incremented by one in the program. Likewise, the compiler will automatically add two to the address used to access an array of ints even though the index only changes by one. The same incrementing to scale holds true when arrays of structures are used; the size of the structure becomes the scale of the array.

The size of arrays, structures, and unions plays a part in how the compiler manages memory addresses when dealing with these types. Every data type you declare has a size and thus a scale associated with that data type's access.

Initializers

The last item of information conveyed to the compiler when a variable is declared is its *initializer*. Unlike other languages that determine a variable's type by giving the variable a value, C depends on the variable's declaration to assign type. Giving a value to a variable (indeed, making space in memory for the variable at all) is handled separately. Initializers are thus an optional part of most declarations. (The only exception is a union's declaration, in which initializers are not allowed.)

Depending on a variable's storage class, the variable may be automatically initialized to zero (by the compiler) before the program starts or may contain random garbage. The former is assured for the external storage class (those declared outside function blocks) and for those marked with the keyword static. The latter applies to variables declared inside function blocks (assumed to be autos) or marked with the keyword register.

You initialize a variable when you assign a value to the variable in the same place as its declaration. The following examples of initializers will help make the format clear:

```
long int whopper = 4324212;
char answer = 'Y';
int true = 1;
double balance = 10000.00;
struct bowling team[] = {
        { 175.65, 123.22, 201.21, 150.23 },
        { 151.21, 162.88, 184.18, 131.62 }};
char *come_on = "What's your sign?";
char select[] = {1,2,4,8};
```

Here the first two elements of the array of bowling structures are being initialized with the four average scores that the team members earned. Because each array element requires four values, the braces surround groups of four. Structures, as well as arrays, are aggregates and require a set of braces around items of the structure's initializing set. Thus, an extra pair of braces surrounds all the items in the bowling example. Because this example is an array of structures, each subgroup is in turn surrounded by braces and separated from one another by commas. The same rule applies to the initialization of the singly dimensioned char array select.

As previously noted, a character string constant enclosed within double quotation marks produces a pointer. The variable char *come_on is therefore initialized with the address at which the compiler placed the string What's your sign?

Initializers like these are presumed to be effective at compile time and can thus be thought to take effect before the program is executed. Therefore, the values used with them must also be known at compile time; that is, they must be constants. It is possible, however, to initialize auto variables with other variables, for example, with the result of a function invocation. The following form shows how:

```
some_function()
{
     int var1 = func2();

     rest of function ...

}
```

The `int` variable `var1` is created during the program's execution and uses temporary storage that will evaporate when the function `some_function` is exited. On entry, the function `func2` is executed, and its returned value is assigned to `var1`. The same sequence of events would not be possible if `var1` had been declared as either a `static` or `extern` variable. In the case of a `static`, because the compiler defines `static` variable space at compile time, the variable returned from the function `func2()` would not be available yet. In the case of a variable marked with the keyword `extern`, the declaration would be for type information only. In other words, such a declaration lets the compiler know that space has been reserved in another module. Where that module is located won't be known until the program modules have been linked together.

When `auto` (or `register`) variables are initialized, the compiler generates the same machine instructions as if the two statements

```
int var1;
var1 = func2();
```

were written in the source code.

Because `auto` variables are created "on the fly" (usually on the stack), initializing `auto` aggregates (array and structure variables declared inside function blocks) is not allowed.

The following rules apply to the use of initializers in declarations:

1. Variables declared with the keyword `extern` may not be initialized.

2. `auto` aggregates (arrays, structures, and `unions` declared within a block) may not be initialized.

3. `static` storage class variables are initialized only once, at the beginning of the program or on first entry into the function.

4. static storage class variables may only be initialized with a value known at compile time.

5. static and external storage class variables are zeroed at the beginning of the program unless they are explicitly initialized.

6. autos are initialized at every function invocation as if each auto's assignment were separate from its declaration.

Two final points about declarations should be made. First, more than one variable may be declared on a line after the type keyword, thus making easier the declaration of several variables of the same type. The type keyword or phrase (such as int, float, or struct tag {declarations}) needs to be written only once, with multiple identifier parts appended and separated by commas. Second, all declarations end with a semicolon. (This requirement is easy to remember because it is common to all C statements.)

1

Other Features of C

So that you don't get the idea that by reading the first chapter, you're ready to apply for a job as a C programmer, this chapter presents some of the more advanced features of C data types. These features include attribute lists, `typedefs`, and casts.

Attribute Lists

An *attribute list* is the sequence of declarations given to an identifier (the variable's name) by a programmer and represents the data that needs to be manipulated. Despite the impression you may have received that a single variable can aspire to be only one type, a variable may be described by combinations of type declarations, all rolled into one, in order to tell the compiler about some complex data structure the programmer has dreamed up. The ability to decipher this list of attributes is an important stepping-stone in understanding C.

Multiply dimensioned arrays have already been mentioned. Such an array is the most straightforward representation of a terminal's screen of 24 rows of 80 characters each. A program designed to move data in and out of a multiply dimensioned array might include the declaration

```
char screen[24][80];
```

which makes the screen a two-dimensional array of characters, 24 rows high by 80 columns wide. The [0][0] element of this array of characters is in the upper left corner, with [23][79] in the bottom right. The leftmost character of each row can be retrieved by using [0][0], [1][0], [2][0], and so on. Figure 1.1 shows the attribute list for the variable screen.

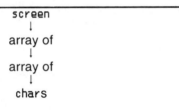

Fig. 1.1. Attribute list for `char screen [24][80];`

A more complicated but equally useful data structure is given by the declaration

```
struct bowling {
      float bowler1;
      float bowler2;
      float bowler3;
      float bowler4;
} team[20];
```

which represents an array of 20 structures (one for every team in a league), each used to hold the average scores of the four players on each team. The members of this structure all happen to be the same type of data: `float`. Access to any player's average on any team n (where 0 <= n <= 19) can be achieved by the statement

```
team[n].bowlerx
```

where x is replaced by 1, 2, 3, or 4, depending on which average is desired. You know that this array consists of 20 structures when you create the attribute list in figure 1.2.

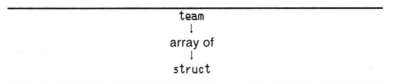

Fig. 1.2. Attribute list for `struct bowling team [20];`

The command line used to initiate a program written in C may in-clude parameters that can be passed to that line. C has a nice way of giving the program access to these commands through a vari-able that is declared by the form

```
char *argv[];   /* argument vector for C program line */
```

Its attribute list is shown in figure 1.3.

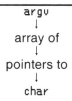

Fig. 1.3. Attribute list for `char *argv[]`;

In figure 1.3, `argv` is described as an array of pointers to `chars`. Because "pointer to `chars`" is the way C manipulates character strings, `*argv[]` is an array of pointers to character strings, each string being a parameter that appeared on the command line. (More about this subject is found in the discussion of `main` in Chapter 2.)

Finally, the following complex variable appears in Part III in a function used with a handy menu selection capability:

```
int (*menu[])();
```

Its attribute list is shown in figure 1.4.

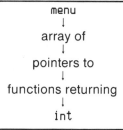

Fig. 1.4. Attribute list for `int (*menu[])();`

Pointers to functions, which define entry points to functions for the compiler, are stored in the array. The function desired will be selected by supplying the array indexes. The value returned from the function, if any, will be interpreted as an `int`. It allows a function to be selected on the basis of an array index.

All these attribute lists were deciphered through the use of the right-left rule.[1] This rule is expressed as an algorithm with eight steps. (See table 1.1.)

---

[1]See Purdum and others for a more complete discussion of this rule and also for the complimentary left-right rule for constructing an attribute declaration, given a data structure.

Table 1.1
The Right-Left Rule

1. Find the identifier, then look . . .

2. To the right for a ")"; if found, skip to 6

3. To the right for "[ ]"; if found, say "an array of . . ." and goto 2

4. To the right for "( )"; if found, say " . . . function(s) returning . . ." and goto 2

5. To the right for a "; ", "=", or ", "; if found, goto 8

6. To the left for an "*"; if found, say " . . . pointer(s) to . . ." and goto 6

7. To the left for a "("; if found, goto 2

8. Say the terminating attribute

Understanding the attribute list of a variable is important because the list reveals the way C interprets the data found in the variable. A common error that occurs (to the chagrin of unsuspecting C programmers) is the misinterpretation of data by the program. This may cause subtle and sometimes catastrophic problems. Along with the power and flexibility of C comes the responsibility of knowing what you're doing and what the compiler is thinking.

A new organization of the same list of data types already introduced can be used to help construct attribute lists. Table 1.2 is divided by the types that *terminate* an attribute list and those that can only be *intermediate*. The distinction is important. A function, for example, cannot return a function. An array of arrays is likewise nonsensical if it ends there; the array must hold something, such as chars or ints. A "pointer to pointer" that doesn't point to anything makes no sense either. Functions, arrays, and pointers are thus intermediate attributes. All other data types are terminating.

Table 1.2 further divides the intermediate types into *right* and *left*. A pointer symbol (*) is the only attribute that can be placed on the left of an identifier; function and array symbols (( ) and [ ]) are always found on the right. (Hierarchy rules govern which symbols bind in what order; these rules are discussed in Chapter 3.)

Only one terminating attribute is allowed per declaration, and this attribute is always written on the left, after the adjectives used to

---

Table 1.2
Variable Attributes

Terminating   Intermediate

char

| int |
| long |
| unsigned |
| short |

float

| double |

| struct |

| union |

left
pointer

right
array
function

---

indicate the variable's scope and storage class, that is, static or extern.

Casts

C offers a means of modifying its default interpretation of a variable's data type during the execution of a program through the action of the *cast* operator. This feature should rightly be grouped with the other operators, but it fits in so nicely here that a brief preview of a cast operator's use is justified.

As previously mentioned, the C compiler is told about every variable used in a program by the variable's declaration. In the following circumstances, however, this method is not appropriate, and a cast operator is recommended:

1. The data is created while the program is running, and therefore neither variable name nor declaration can be used to tell the compiler what type of data will be found in a variable.

2. The data in a particular variable changes while the program is running, thus requiring a change in the variable's interpretation.

(This application might otherwise be a candidate for use of a union.)

Casts typically appear in code that handles more complex data structures. Casts allow the programmer to replace temporarily a variable's default attribute list (assigned to the variable when the program was compiled) with a new list. How this is done is described in Chapter 2. Several functions in Part III make use of this important capability.

Typedefs

A convenience provided by C when you are dealing with common attribute declarations is the typedef. This feature allows an arbitrarily complex data type, normally declared with a combination of attributes, to be renamed as a single, new type. A typedef can be used throughout a program in place of the more complex attribute list. The example in table 1.3 will make the use of typedefs a little clearer.

Table 1.3
Result of Using typedef

Before	After

`typedef struct file_io {`
`        int file_descriptor;`
`        int chars_left;`
`        int mode;`
`        char *next_char;`
`        chat *buffer;`
`} *FILE;`
	`FILE mine;`

File I/O in C is accomplished by using a function that needs to know certain information, such as location of the file buffer, characters in the buffer, and access mode. This information is made known to the function by passing it a pointer to a structure containing the variables that the function needs. The requirement is so common that instead of continuing to declare a somewhat lengthy list of attributes every time file I/O is needed, you can create a simple new type called FILE. This facility also adds clarity to a program because the new name often says more about what the data type is used for than does the complex declaration that the typedef replaces.

The Before column describes the identifier FILE, which may be used in place of the declaration it follows: pointer to struct, with an organization as shown and with the tag file_io. The keyword typedef prevents the compiler from assuming that the identifier is a variable for which the compiler must reserve space.

The typedef FILE can be used in the declaration, as shown in the After column, to define the variable mine as a pointer to struct, with an organization described by file_io, where space for the pointer will be reserved. The programmer not only has made very clear that the variable is used with file access, but also has made life simpler. (Question: Does mine point to anything yet? Answer: Not until it is given a value; mine just makes space for an address and prepares the program to interpret what is at that address as a data structure with these members.)

In the following form, a typedef is used to create two "new" types that some programmers prefer to use:

```
typedef unsigned int BOOL, VOID;
```

Now the use of the types BOOL and VOID will be accepted in declarations such as

```
BOOL ready;
VOID wait();
```

The declarations will inform anyone trying to maintain this program that the variable ready and the variable returned from the function wait are each something more than an unsigned int. The variable ready likely produces only true or false values by its declaration as a Boolean type. And the function wait probably returns nothing by being declared VOID. (This typedef would only be used if the compiler you were using didn't include VOID as a reserved keyword.)

Typedefs are also valuable because they can produce new types that can legally be used with the cast operator (and C's sizeof() feature, as you'll see later).

Constants and Resolved Data Types

The following discussion of constants introduces a feature they share with variables: resolved data types. (These will receive more attention shortly.) Constants are values that never change in a program. Constants don't have names, and they don't need declarations. However, constants may be used to give a variable an initial value, as in

```
int variable = 2;
```

or to compare to a variable, as in

```
if(variable < 2)
```

where some action will take place based on the outcome of the test. (In both these examples, the constant value is 2.)

The compiler imposes a declaration on a constant from the way the constant is written and from its value. The interpretation is very straightforward, as indicated in table 1.4.

Table 1.4
Interpretation of Constants

2	int
1287	int
10.5	double
12L	long
-1234.23444	double
32768	long
'a'	character
"Hello, world"	pointer
0.	double
0765	octal int
0x1ACFD	hex long
123498765	long
'\007'	character
'\n'	character

Note that C allows the use of three number bases: octal, decimal, and hex. Decimal numbers are always assumed. Octal numbers are indicated with a leading zero. And hex numbers are formed by using a leading 0x.

Constants exist in only five flavors, as indicated in table 1.4: char, int, double, long, and pointer to char. Four of these are known as resolved types: int, double, long, and pointer. Why does C, on the one hand, offer such flexibility in the combination and declaration of complex data types and, on the other hand, impose these limitations? The answer is efficiency.

For any given variable, the C compiler must generate the correct machine instructions so that it can manipulate the variable's contents properly. We've already seen how the compiler relies on a variable's declaration, and on the way a constant is written, to determine how to select these instructions. So that a limited repertoire of variable manipulation schemes needs to be "taught" to the compiler, the compiler automatically converts some variable types into others before it deals with them. The types the compiler chooses are called *resolved* types.

In the case of constants, the resolved type is selected by application of the following rules:

1. The value of a number predetermines a type based on its size; all assumptions assume a signed representation.

2. A decimal point forces a double.

3. An int can be forced into a long by appending an l or L.

4. A constant of type pointer to char is created by the use of double quotation marks (" "). The characters can be thought to occupy an initialized array of chars.

Type Conversions

C allows many different types of data to be used in programs so that arbitrarily complex data structures can be created and manipulated as demanded by the application. The language, however, performs three types of conversions on variables either automatically or at the programmer's request. (See table 1.5.)

Table 1.5
Type Conversions

Automatic
1. Promotion, to limit the ways variables are passed to or returned from functions, or produced from expressions
2. Type balancing, when operators join variables of different types

Forced
3. Assignment, when one type is forced into another

These conversions make the compiler simpler to implement and add efficiencies in the way machine instructions are used to accomplish the intent of the programmer. As you might predict, a more efficient program is one that minimizes the conversions required.

Promotion

Promotion occurs when a variable of a smaller type is promoted to a larger type. Each of the smaller types listed in table 1.6 is always converted to the larger type before being passed to functions as parameters, before being returned from functions, or as the result of the evaluation of an expression. The long and int types are also resolved types.

Table 1.6
Promotion Paths

Normal type	Resolved type
char short	int
float	double

Type Balancing

The second form of conversion is required when variables of different types meet in expressions. Here the rules (see table 1.7) are quite logical; predictably, the smaller type gets promoted to match the larger type before the operation is performed. If the value produced by the expression is bigger than the largest type, however, a loss of data results.

Conversion by Assignment

The last form of conversion (see the rules in table 1.8) occurs when an assignment statement forces a larger variable into a smaller one. In this case, the programmer has to be sure that the effects of truncation are unimportant because information is always lost.

Now you know why numeric constants are created in only three flavors (int, long, double): to avoid as much conversion overhead as possible when constants meet variables.

Table 1.7
Type Balancing Conversion Rules

1. Convert `chars` and `short ints` → `int` (sign extended)
2. Convert `floats` → `double` (zero padded)
3. If any operand is a `double`, all → `double`; `double` is the type of the result; goto 7
4. If any operand is a `long`, all → `long`; `long` is the type of the result; goto 7
5. If any operand is an `unsigned int`, all → `unsigned int`; `unsigned int` is the type of the result; goto 7
6. Else, both operands must be `int`; `int` is the type of the result
7. Done

Table 1.8
Assignment Conversion Rules

1. `int` → `char`, `short int` (most significant bits truncated)
2. `double` → `float` (rounded before truncation)

There is a *character constant* type which C provides so that single characters (rather than small numeric values) can be defined as constants and not take up the room that an `int` takes. These character constants are formed by placing a single quotation mark in front of and behind the character desired. Table 1.9 shows three forms of character constants allowed.

Now you have a passing understanding of how C programs are built from separately compiled files with one or more functions, and how scope and storage class affect the privacy and life span of variables used by those functions. You also know about the different data types available in C, what kind and size of variables each type can store, and how variables are declared and combined. To understand how C programs work, you need to know how this information is applied. We'll see in the next chapter, therefore, what the pieces look like when they're put together.

Table 1.9
Character Constants

ʹ x ʹ   where x is any printable ASCII character

ʹ \x ʹ   where x is chosen from the following characters to represent the special feature:

        n = a newline
        t = a tab
        \ = a backslash
        b = a backspace
        " = a double quotation mark
           (used in a string)
        ʹ = a single quotation mark
           (used as a char constant)
        r = a carriage return
        f = form feed

ʹ \xxx ʹ   where xxx is any octal number chosen to represent any 8-bit value

Part II

What C Programs Look Like

When you pick up a C program listing, start looking at the big pieces first: modules, functions, and variable declarations. Later, you can turn your attention to what happens to the data inside the modules and functions. The purpose of this section of the book is to help you understand the facilities C provides for manipulating that data. Part II is titled "What C Programs Look Like" because the preprocessor directives, function definitions, flow control statements, and expressions create a picture that can be understood and appreciated much like art. Some details are subtle; others are obvious. Many constructions are straightforward; a few require close study. The more you look, the more you see (no pun intended).

The best programs start off with a title block or some other descriptive heading, telling what the name of the program is, what it does, what version it is (and the date last modified), what functions are included in the program, who wrote it, and what bugs or deficiencies remain. If the source file (or module) is part of a larger program, the module should include information about its relationship to the whole program. You may also find information about how to compile the module, what compiler switches should be used, and how to link the module with other modules to make a program that works the way the author intended.

Naturally, the compiler requires none of this information. It is included to let you and others know as much as possible about what the author was trying to do, and to make easier the job of fixing problems or adding features later. The *comments* appear between a pair of the most common symbols in C: a /* before the comment and an */ afterward. This pair of symbols tells the compiler to ignore everything between them.

2

Inside a C Program

Preprocessor Directives

Before you ever reach any real C code, you will most likely run into special statements that are called *preprocessor directives*. The term implies that something gets done before the real compiler kicks in, and that is exactly what happens. Four types of preprocessor directives may be used. Each one begins with the symbol # (in column one), which is pronounced by saying "pound" or "number" before the word that follows the symbol, as shown in this list of preprocessor directives:

```
#include "filename"

#include <filename>

#define identifier replacement-text

#define identifier(argument)
          macro-expansion

#undef identifier

#if constant-expression

#ifdef identifier

#ifndef identifier

#else
```

```
#endif
```

```
#line constant identifier
```

Preprocessor directives do not require final semicolons as other C statements do.

#include

The #include preprocessor directive allows the programmer to write a block of code once, place it in a separate #include file, and have it included in many source files. This directive is most often used to allow in one place the declaration of different variables and constants that may be used in several modules. In this way, changes can be effected in all the modules by changing their common #include files. The directive not only minimizes typing but also reduces the risk of errors that may occur when you retype the variables and constants required into each source file.

You will notice that most C programs, and particularly those that perform file I/O, include a file named stdio.h. This file provides definitions of constants and data types required by other functions and included in the standard library. By using a #include file to make these definitions a part of your source file, you are assured that what is needed will be there and will be correct.[1]

The only difference between the use of "filename" and <filename> lies in where the preprocessor looks for the file (in the computer's file directory). In some operating systems, most notably UNIX, a special place is dedicated for the storage of such files (in UNIX, typically the "/usr/include" directory). The <filename> notation is used to find the file there. Otherwise, the use of "filename" usually retrieves the file from the current working directory.

#define, #undef

The #define directive comes in two flavors, with a third to #undefine what you've #defined. The first is similar to a text editor's search-and-replace feature. The second provides a formula into which variables can be inserted and produces a result. The third simply makes the compiler forget that an identifier was #defined to mean anything in the first place.

---

[1]stdio.h files from four popular C microcomputer compilers are included in Part III.

A #define tells the preprocessor to replace all occurrences of the identifier with the *replacement-text* prior to compilation. A program can be better understood with this provision because it allows the use of names like CONTROL_PORT, EOF, and ERROR instead of their numeric equivalents. Names convey more information than numbers. Some programmers prefer to use identifiers wherever numeric constants would be used. You will find that most identifiers are capitalized to highlight their use in the program, but capitalizing them is not a requirement. Each of the following examples uses #define to replace numeric constants with readable names:

```
#define EOF -1
#define CONTROL_PORT 0xa0
```

Because a #define can be used with just about any replacement-text, this preprocessor directive can also be used to create shorthand references to complex or long expressions. For example, if a reference to a structure member becomes unwieldy because of multiple indirections, as in

```
struct_ptr1->struct_ptr2->member
```

then the use of

```
#define PTR struct_ptr1->struct_ptr2
```

will allow the same member to be accessed by writing

```
PTR->member
```

For another example of the application of #define, consider the statement

```
#define VOID int
```

whose replacement provides the same facility described under typedefs, but in a different way. Here the preprocessor replaces occurrences of the string VOID with int. As before, VOID may be used to declare a function, but here the compiler has not been told about a new data type. The compiler sees only the int that replaced VOID after the preprocessor's job was done. In this case the effect is the same. (Note: The use of a #define is not always a replacement for a typedef. Consider a more complex typedef like FILE.)

The inclusion of arguments within a #define turns it into a *parameterized macro*. Such a macro provides a powerful means to replace a possibly complex expression with a simple one and to avoid the overhead (extra machine instructions) associated with a function invocation. Like the simple replacement version, the identifier is typically capitalized. Each of the following examples uses a #define with one argument (parameterized macros) to convert inches to centimeters and Fahrenheit to Celsius:

```
#define INCH_CM(x) (x * 2.54)
#define FAHR_CENT(x) ((x - 32) * 5.0 / 9.0)
```

Note: There may be more than one argument so long as you use different argument symbols.

In the program source, the line

```
temp = FAHR_CENT(var1);
```

is replaced by the preprocessor with

```
temp = ((var1 - 32) * 5.0 / 9.0);
```

prior to the compiler pass.

Note the heavy use of parentheses in the replacement-text. This practice is common. In places where the text is to be inserted, the grouping of variables with adjacent operators should be planned and not left to chance.

As previously mentioned, the #undef directive is used to "forget" a definition for an identifier. This directive may not appear immediately useful. Its primary application is with the conditional compilation directives described in the next section.

#if, #ifdef, and #ifndef

#if, #ifdef, and #ifndef provide conditional compilation. This series of directives allows the programmer to write parts of a program that the compiler can or cannot "see," depending on the value of a constant expression or identifier. The source code following a #if will compile if the result produced from the evaluation of a constant expression is nonzero, that is, true.

Many programs use conditional compilation so that one source module can be configured at compile time for a variety of situations. Giving "multiple personalities" to a single module enables bug fixes or enhancements to be made to one module rather than many. A liability of conditional compilation, however, is that it can make the source code more difficult to understand.

A typical example occurs when you allow a module responsible for terminal-dependent functions to be conditionally compilable for one of several terminals. Consider the following:

```
#define TRUE 1              /* just to make it clear  */
#define FALSE 0             /* true and false are below */

#define ADM3A FALSE         /* only one of these      */
#define TVI910 TRUE         /* can be set TRUE        */
#define WYSE50 FALSE
#define IBMPC FALSE

clear()                     /* clear screen and home  */
{                           /* cursor                 */
#if TVI910 | WYSE50
        putchar(0x1b);      /* an escape              */
        putchar('*');
#else
    #if ADM3A
            putchar(0x1a);  /* a cntrl-Z              */
    #else
            putchar(0x1b);  /* for the IBM PC using   */
            putchar('[');   /* ANSI.SYS */
            putchar('2');   /* sends 'ESC [ 2 J'      */
            putchar('J');
    #endif
#endif
}
```

Here the #if has been used to "turn on" the section of code pertaining to the TVI910 terminal. The source code that would clear the screen and home the cursor for the ADM3A and IBM PC has effectively been "turned off." Since the TVI910 and WYSE50 use the same clear-screen code, their values have been OR'd together to allow one piece of source to serve both the TVI910 and the WYSE50. (The Boolean OR operator, |, will be discussed in Chapter 3.) Notice that one #if construction has been placed inside another. This procedure is called *nesting* of conditionals and is common when more than a two-way choice must be made.

The subject of constant expressions will be presented in more detail once operators and expressions have been introduced. For the moment, just consider that the true/false (nonzero/zero) value resulting from a constant expression can be produced from almost any formula whose values are known at compile time.

The code following a #ifdef will compile if its identifier has been used with a preceding #define directive. The #ifndef works in exactly the opposite way, allowing compilation of the code as long as the identifier has not been #defined (or, as already indicated, if the identifier's definition has been forgotten with #undef).

If you instead wrote

```
clear()
{
#ifdef ADDS
     putchar(0xc);        /* a cntrl-L for the ADDS   */
#else
     putchar(0x1a);       /* a cntrl-Z for the ADM3A  */
#endif
}
```

you would produce a clear-screen code for the ADM3A because no #define ADDS appears. Note that the clear-screen code for the ADDS would be produced even if it were #defined FALSE!

The use of #else always occurs in combination with one of the #ifs. The #else allows the section of code that follows to be compiled if the previous section was not, thus implementing a simple two-way decision. In all cases of conditional compilation, the end of the block must be marked by #endif.

#line

Finally, the #line directive lets the programmer take control over the line number and file name that the compiler's error-reporting facility uses to announce problems. This feature is not implemented in many compilers and has marginal utility for most programmers.

Even though we have not yet generated any code, declared any variables, or performed any work, our sample C program looks like this thus far:

```
/*  title: my_program
 *
 *  author: Kim Brand
 *  version: 1.0    date:  May 7, 1984
 *
 *  bugs: it doesn't do anything, no functions
 */
```

```
#include "stdio.h"        /* we need file I/O   */
#include "math.h"         /* and math constants */

#define READ 0            /* just for the file  */
#define WRITE 1           /* I/O mode           */
#define BUFFER_SIZE 128   /* data block size    */

#define PI 3.1415926535   /* pi to adequate prc */

#define DEG_RAD(x) ((360 / (2 * PI))*x)
                          /* deg from radians   */
```

What Declarations Look Like

When declarations were introduced in Chapter 0, you saw how important they were in letting the C compiler know what variables would be used in a program, as well as in providing information about a variable's scope, storage class, type, scale, and possibly initial value. Most C programmers put their declarations for all external storage class variables in the immediate source module *after* the preprocessor directives. Sometimes declarations are #included.

Remember not to declare again the variables already declared in a #include file. Pay attention also to the differences in declaring a variable, defining it (making space for it), and possibly giving it an initial value. A structure declared in a #include file with

```
struct tag {
     int member1;
     float member2;
};
```

reserves no memory. The structure needs to be combined with an identifier in one of the modules, as in

```
struct tag name;
```

before memory space is allocated for its members to occupy. In a similar manner another module that needs access to the same variable would #include the same file but have a statement like

```
extern struct tag name;
```

Variables defined elsewhere, but #included and used in the immediate source module, must be marked with the extern keyword.

Keep in mind also that just declaring a variable and reserving space for it do not give the variable any usable value—that of a pointer, in particular.

What Functions Look Like

Now let's see how functions look and work within a program. The following sections examine how functions are declared, how parameters get in and out of functions, how variables used inside a function are declared, and how the special function main is used.

All functions have the form

```
[static] [type] function_name (parameters, if any)
parameter declarations, if any
{ opening brace

    declarations for local variables, if any

    action statements

} closing brace
```

Unless otherwise declared, a function's type is presumed to be int, which is actually the type of the value that the function returns, if any. The function may be declared with another terminating type near where the function is defined (that is, where its executable code is), or with other external declarations, such as

```
type function_name();
```

A common function included in most standard libraries is sqrt(). As the name suggests, this function returns the square root of its single passed parameter. Since square roots typically include decimal fractions, sqrt() is designed to return a double. The program in which the function is used must be told about this noninteger type by a declaration such as

```
double sqrt();
```

If forgotten, the value returned will be assumed to be an int, and results from the use of the sqrt() function will be misinterpreted.

The name of the function must be unique for the first few characters so that the function will not be confused with other external storage class variables or functions. The exact number of significant characters depends on the compiler/linker used, but the number is usually eight or less. In addition, the upper- and lower-case distinction that C makes regarding identifiers may be lost by the assembler or the linker (if used). Check your C compiler documentation for clarification on this subject.

Immediately following the name is an opening parenthesis and the list of parameters that the function was passed to do its job. As already indicated, these values are copies of the variables sent there by the parent function and therefore may not be affected directly by what happens in this function. No parameters may be needed by the function, in which case the closing parenthesis follows immediately. The list given here is position dependent; that is, the order of the variables must match the order of the variables in the parent. On the other hand, any names can be used for these parameters because they will be private to the function. Good practice dictates that the names chosen give some indication as to what they are or how they will be used.

A special function, `main`, is used to indicate where the program begins. This function may appear in any module and, within the module, in any sequence with other functions. Most C compilers insert an initializing routine at the program's beginning which jumps to `main` for the start of the program's executable code.

As previously mentioned, parameters from the command line can be passed to the program at this point. The following form of the `main` function accomplishes this purpose:

```
main(argc, argv)
int argc;
char *argv[];
{
    rest of 'main' function here
}
```

The `argc` parameter is a count of how many white-space-delimited words (character strings) were included on the command line used to execute the program. This parameter is at least one, as the program's name is counted. An array of pointers to these words is available through the variable `argv`. Following is a brief example to show what happens:

```
A>progname infile outfile <cr>
```

The initialization routine that the C compiler executes before the start of the program `progname` sets up the `argc` and `argv` parameters like this:

```
argc = 3;
```

```
argv[0] is a pointer to progname
argv[1] is a pointer to infile
argv[2] is a pointer to outfile
```

On the next line, and before the opening brace, come declarations for the parameters passed to the function. Because any function depends on knowing what type of data the function is being passed in order to make use of that data, the declarations must match the data types declared in the parent function. The order here is unimportant, but the names used must match those between the parentheses. If a variable is not declared, it will be assumed to be an int, but declaring every variable is the recommended practice.

A style issue is at stake regarding placement of the opening brace. Most programmers place it on the line below, as shown in the previous example, or a tab stop in from the left. C doesn't care. The only important criteria to consider are legibility and consistency. The closing brace is usually placed on a line by itself but can also be found left-justified or indented. (To improve readability, some programmers #define the words BEGIN and END to replace { and }, respectively.) The closing brace, matched with the opening one at the beginning of the function, marks the end of the function. The closing brace performs the same duty as a RETURN in a subroutine. (You'll soon see that in C the keyword return can be used to get back before the closing brace is reached and/or to send back some value to the parent function.)

The declarations for variables used inside the function must precede any action statements and are usually separated from them by a blank line. Most programmers indent all text within the braces to give a visual cue about what is inside the function block and then continue to indent to a new level for each block within the function. (This format will be described later in Chapter 4, Flow Control.)

These declarations, made within a function block, will produce variables that are private to the function. If the keyword static is used in a variable's declaration, space will be reserved for the variable at compile time, and the variable may be initialized to a value by the programmer. Otherwise, the variable has a default value of zero. This static value can be assumed to be there the first time the function is invoked, but whatever value is left there when the function is completed will be there on reentry.

The compiler will assume that the storage class of the variable is
auto. autos may be initialized as well (except for aggregates), but
the effect is the same as if the variable were declared, and in a different statement, given some value. In other words, the variable will
take on the initialized value with each invocation of the function. If
not initialized, auto (and register) variables have garbage on entry
and lose whatever value they had on exit.

Last come the action statements, which perform the work that gets
done in a C program. These statements can be divided into two
categories: expressions and flow control statements. Expressions
are discussed in the next chapter, and flow control is the subject
of Chapter 4.

3
Expressions

Expressions are perhaps the most wonderful thing about C. You may have detected references to expressions in the preceding text without finding a definition. Here is one:

> An *expression* consists of variables, constants, functions, or subexpressions (operands) on or between which operators (unary, binary, and ternary) act according to the rules of hierarchy to produce a resolved data type and value.

This definition includes a reference to operators and hierarchy rules. There are three classes of operators: unary, binary, and ternary. These operators work with one, two, or three operands, respectively. They each produce one of two possible results: numeric or logical. And numeric results come in two varieties: arithmetic and Boolean (bitwise).

You are probably familiar with most of the symbols C uses for its operators (for example, +, -, *, <, and =). But some symbols of equal importance may be new to you, such as !, ==, &&, and ||. Each of these symbols is listed in the hierarchy rules (see table 3.1) with a brief description of what the symbol does. The functions in Part III provide many examples of how these symbols are used and combined. Some of the more unusual ones are given special attention afterward.

Although you may be more familiar with expressions involving variables, some brief but important points should be made about expressions involving constants, that is, constant expressions.

Constant expressions were mentioned in the discussion of the #if preprocessor directive. These expressions also played a role in the use of initializers, and they will be used in the switch flow control statement, covered later in Chapter 4.

: Both 2nd and 3rd expressions must be of same resolved/promoted type, or pointer and 0.

14. `=` `+=` `-=` `*=` `/=` `%=` `>>=` `<<=` `&=` `|=` `^=` ←
Note: Left operand is replaced by itself and result of operation with right operand in all but =.

15. Sequence operator `,` →
Rightmost expression becomes type and value.

The subgroup of expressions that constitutes allowable constant expressions is created by applying the following restrictions:

1. Constant expressions must involve values known at compile time (including values produced by `sizeof`).

2. Constant expressions can use only the following numeric operators:

+	addition	-	unary minus
-	subtraction	&	Boolean AND
*	multiplication	I	Boolean OR
/	division	^	Boolean XOR
%	remainder (modulus)	~	Boolean NOT
<<	shift left	>>	shift right
?:	two-way choice		

Or these logical operators:

==	equal to	!=	not equal to
<	less than	>	greater than
<=	less than or equal to	>=	greater than or equal to

Statements

When an expression stands alone in a program, the expression is called a *statement*. A statement, then, is an expression followed by a semicolon. Statements usually involve assignments or function invocations. Like functions, statements may be found in blocks, that is, grouped within opening and closing braces ({ and }). These blocks maintain the same rules regarding scope that were previously mentioned for function blocks.[1] Statements will take on more significance later when flow control is discussed in Chapter 4.

A peculiar statement for which you will later find a use is the *null* statement. This "do nothing" curiosity is nevertheless important for those cases in which doing nothing is exactly what should be done. Its form is

;

which should be easy to remember.

---

[1] See Alan Feuer's *C Puzzle Book* (Prentice-Hall, 1982), especially the section on storage classes, for some interesting manifestations of these C features.

Precedence

The hierarchy table (table 3.1) is organized by rows, from top to bottom, in order of operator precedence. If operators from different rows are found in the same expression, they form subexpressions with their nearest operand neighbors. Each subexpression is evaluated in the order dictated by the rules of hierarchy, with the subexpression's result feeding adjacent subexpressions that are evaluated, in turn, until each is evaluated and a resolved type and value are all that are left. The result "bubbles up" to take the place of the expression in the program.

The distinction between logical and numeric results is important. (Logical operators are highlighted in the table.) C interprets non-zero values as logical true and zero values as logical false. Sub-expressions in which logical operators are used can produce one of only two results: a 1 if the subexpression evaluates true, and a Ø if it evaluates false. In the expression

    1 < 2

the result of the expression is 1. In the expression

    2 < 1

the result is Ø. The resulting 1 or Ø may be used as either a logical or a numeric input to another subexpression; C doesn't care. The type of a logical result is int.

Most programmers indicate the order in which they intend an expression to be evaluated by using parentheses if confusion is likely or if the order of evaluation is important. When order is a factor, the evaluation of a subexpression is said to have "side effects" because a variable affected within the subexpression is used again in another subexpression within the same expression.[2] For very complex expressions, multiple levels of parentheses are sometimes required. The simple example

    var1 * var2 - var3

is treated as two subexpressions evaluated in the order

    var1 * var2

    produces intermediate result: temp

---

[2] From Kernighan and Ritchie, Appendix A, Section 7: "Expressions involving . . . *, +, &, |, [or] ^ . . . may be rearranged arbitrarily, even in the presence of parentheses; to force a particular order of evaluation an explicit temporary [variable] must be used."

which is then used in the subexpression

```
temp - var3
```

which replaces the original subexpression in the statement in which it was found.

For expressions with more than one operator from the same row of the hierarchy table, a different technique is used to resolve what gets done first. On the right of the group of operators in each row is one of two motion symbols: ←, which means "right to left"; or →, which means "left to right." These symbols represent the direction in which the compiler, while scanning the whole expression, evaluates subexpressions formed with operators of the same row. In a complex expression, with operators from different rows and more than one operator from within a row, the subexpressions with operators from different rows will be evaluated according to the hierarchy rules in table 3.1. Then the remaining subexpressions, with operators from the same row, will be evaluated "left to right" or "right to left."

To examine a more complex example, consider the following expression (math mavens will recognize this as one root of a quadratic equation):

```
x = (-b + sqrt(b * b - 4 * a * c)) /2 * a
```

The placement of parentheses and the rules of hierarchy (can you find all nine operators?) allow us to predict how the compiler will treat this expression. The innermost parentheses cause

```
(b * b - 4 * a * c)
```

to be evaluated first. Since the multiplication operator is the higher one here, it will be performed first. Multiplication is evaluated "left to right"; therefore, the order of evaluation of the subexpressions is

```
b * b produces temp1
4 * a produces temp2
temp2 * c replaces temp2
```

Then the following subtraction operator can finally be used:

```
temp1 - temp2 replaces temp1
```

Now temp1 can be passed as a parameter to the function sqrt, which will return a value. Let's allow the value to replace temp1, which can be used in what is left of the expression

```
x = (-b + temp1) / 2 * a
```

Here again, the following subexpression within the parentheses takes a priority in the evaluation order:

```
(-b + temp1)
```

And within the parentheses the unary minus becomes the higher-precedence operator. The order of evaluation is thus

-1 * b produces temp2
temp2 + temp1 replaces temp1

which leaves

```
x = temp1 / 2 * a
```

The rules of hierarchy place multiplication and division on the same level, and both are placed above the assignment operator =. Multiplication and division operators are evaluated "left to right," but in this case the order doesn't matter because any evaluation gives the same result. (Remember the commutative law? However, integer math loses precision during division; this loss of precision can affect results based on what gets done first.) The final evaluation takes place as follows:

temp1 / 2 replaces temp1
temp1 * a replaces temp1
x gets the value of temp1

Note that because of the rules of assignment, x can only accept a value in the range allowed by its type. Since the other parts of the calculation have been performed with variables and constants promoted to double, x had better be the same, or a loss of precision is bound to result.

Many factors touched on earlier now begin to come into play. One factor is the resolved data type. Because C performs arithmetic in only a few resolved data types, subexpressions are evaluated with operands that have been promoted if necessary. Also relevant is the concept of *type balancing*, which ensures that operands of different types are promoted to the type of the largest operand. You can now see how binding affects the use of operators introduced earlier with pointers, arrays, structures, and unions.

The use of many of the operators in the hierarchy table is obvious. Almost every reference source cited discusses them in detail, and we therefore won't spend time on all of them here. The less well-known logical, Boolean, numeric, and assignment operators will be briefly explained for the benefit of those who are not familiar with them. An excellent treatment of operators can be found in Feuer's *C Puzzle Book* (Prentice-Hall, 1982).

Logical Operators

The logical negation operator ! produces a false (∅) result from a true (nonzero) subexpression. Likewise, this operator produces a true (1) result from a false (∅) subexpression. As previously mentioned, the result produced from the use of any logical operator can only be 1 or ∅.

Two very important and frequently used logical operators are those used to test equality and inequality: == and !=, respectively. Beginning programmers, in particular, fail to use the == where it should be used almost as often as they forget to end statements with a semicolon. The operator for testing for equality is typically confused with the assignment operator =. The == produces a logical true or false result; the = merely assigns the value of the expression on its right to the variable on its left. In the example

```
while(x = 1)
    do something
```

the loop will continue forever because at each commencement of the cycle, x is made equal to one, a nonzero value. And something always gets done if the expression between the parentheses is true. What the programmer meant was

```
while(x == 1)
    do something
```

which will stop doing something as soon as x is not equal to 1 (a condition that is presumably affected by doing something).

The logical operators && (AND) and I I (OR) provide a means to test for the truth of *all* subexpressions or *at least one*, respectively, in expressions that involve compound logical subexpressions. To understand these principles clearly, consider the example

```
while((var1 < var2) && (var3 > var4))
    do something
```

which says that something should be done if the results of *both* logical subexpressions (var1 < var2) *and* (var3 > var4) are true. Likewise

```
while((var1 < var2) || (var3 > var4))
     do something
```

allows something to be done if *either* the subexpression (var1 < var2) *or* (var3 > var4) is true.

Notice in these examples that although parentheses are included, they are not required because the precedence of > and < is higher than that of && and ||.

If in the first example the subexpression (var1 < var2) had been evaluated as false, there would have been no need to evaluate the second subexpression. In the second example the result of (var3 > var4) would have been moot if the first subexpression had evaluated as true. C specifically guarantees that these irrelevant subsequent tests will not be made. This feature is an important one to remember when analyzing the side effects of the evaluation of subexpressions with variables that may be used elsewhere in the expression or later in the program.

For example, in the loop

```
while(end < STOP && (start = start + 1) > BEGIN)
     do something
```

the subexpression wrapped by the parentheses is perfectly legal. The subexpression end < STOP is evaluated first, and if it is found to be false, the second subexpression, (start = start + 1) > BEGIN, is *not* evaluated. Therefore, start will not be incremented. Similarly, if the && were replaced by a ||, the second subexpression would not be evaluated if the first is found to be true. Note that the parentheses make no difference.

Boolean Operators

The Boolean operators are named after George Boole (1815-1865), an English mathematician and logician who developed a branch of mathematics based on the properties of binary number systems. These operators deal exclusively with the integer variables char, int, and long. Boolean operators are sometimes called *bitwise* operators because they give the programmer the ability to affect single bits in a variable's binary representation within the computer.

The Boolean NOT operator, ~ (a tilde), turns the ones into zeros and the zeros into ones for every bit in the number. NOT is unary and thus affects only one operand. Don't confuse this operator with the unary minus; a -1 is not the same as ~1. Also don't confuse the action of ~ with ! Whereas !1 equals false (∅), ~1 can be 65534 if interpreted as an unsigned int; otherwise, ~1 is interpreted as -2.

A typical use for the Boolean NOT operator is to create negative logic bit values. For example, floppy disk drives are selected by setting one line of four to a TTL logic low level. A program might use the value 1 to represent drive A and the value 2 to represent drive B, but send ~1 and ~2 (creating 11111110 and 11111101 binary, respectively) to the drive select I/O port to produce the drive select signal.

The Boolean AND, EXCLUSIVE OR (XOR), and OR operators (&, ^, and |, respectively) are binary and require two operands. These operators give C the "bit twiddling" capability of their assembler language counterparts. The operators are typically found in programs that do real-world I/O or that compress more than one piece of information into a single integer. The truth tables included here (see table 3.2) will be familiar only to those reared in such curious pursuits.

Table 3.2
Summary of Boolean Operations

NOT ~	AND &	OR |	XOR ^
~ ∅ = 1 ~ 1 = ∅	∅ & ∅ = ∅ ∅ & 1 = ∅ 1 & ∅ = ∅ 1 & 1 = 1	∅ | ∅ = ∅ ∅ | 1 = 1 1 | ∅ = 1 1 | 1 = 1	∅ ^ ∅ = ∅ ∅ ^ 1 = 1 1 ^ ∅ = 1 1 ^ 1 = ∅

The binary Boolean operators allow a programmer to "mask" bits (with AND), "set" bits (with OR), and "toggle" bits (with XOR). An AND operation will mask (make a zero) any bit of an integer that has a zero in either operand. An OR operation will set (make a 1) any bit of an integer that has a 1 in either operand. And an XOR operation will toggle (make a 1 out of a ∅ or a ∅ out of a 1) any bit of an integer that has a 1 in either operand.

Keep in mind that these operators do not change either of their operands. The operators produce an intermediate result that may be used as is or passed along as the result of a subexpression evaluated as part of a larger expression. Saving this result requires assigning it to another variable or to one of the operands itself. (Assignment operators will be discussed shortly.)

Numeric Operators

The unary *pre-* and *post-increment* (++) and *pre-* and *post-decrement* (--) operators were included in C to acknowledge the special case when the number one (1) is added to or subtracted from a variable. Most computers have an inherent ability (as part of the assembly language instruction set) to increment and decrement any number that can fit into a register or be referenced in memory as a single unit.

C not only provides a special way to increment or decrement a variable by one, but also allows the effect of the operation to be used in the subexpression normally, or to be postponed until the original value has been used in the evaluation of the rest of the expression.

The following examples will help you understand how these operators work. Don't be intimidated. They are always a cause of confusion if you are trying to figure out when a loop stops or what value a variable has at the end of a cycle.

The post-incrementing form

```
x++;
```

and the pre-incrementing form

```
++x;
```

simply increment x by one. These forms are the same as

```
x = x + 1;
```

The advantages to using the pre- and post- forms are that they are easier to read (for some), and they may allow the compiler to choose a more efficient (faster or shorter, or both) sequence of machine instructions to accomplish incrementing and decrementing. The same is true of the pre-decrementing form

```
--x;
```

and the post-decrementing form

```
x--;
```

Both of these forms are identical to

```
x = x - 1;
```

In none of the above cases are the pre- and post- natures of these operators important because there are no related expressions or tests. In other words, the variable x has no role as a subexpression in the evaluation of other local subexpressions.

Many loops, however, take the form

```
while(x--)
     do something
```

which says to continue to do something while x is nonzero, that is, true. If you assume that x is 1 before it is tested this time, what happens next?

The -- post-decrements x because the operator is placed after the variable name. Thus, the test made is against an expression value of 1, and something does get performed this time! The value of x is now zero (∅) for any other use. On the next cycle, x is decremented again, this time to -1, but the value tested against is zero (∅), and therefore something gets passed by. If a pre-decrementing form had been used, the something would have been passed by on the first cycle because the test would have been against a zero—which is the immediate effect of the pre-decrementing operator.

The unary cast operator (type) is an attribute list included within parentheses and used to modify or create a declaration for a variable or expression. This operator may be used in an expression such as

```
(char)variable
```

to force the program to interpret the data at variable as a char, regardless of the way the variable was originally declared. Likewise, the expression

```
(int *)message
```

forces the program to treat the value at message as a pointer to int.

The unary *address of* operator (&) is used to obtain the address where a variable is located in memory. This operator may be used to initialize a pointer variable with the address of something, as in the example

```
int var1;
```

which declares an integer variable and makes a place (defines space) for the variable in memory. And the declaration

```
int *ptr;
```

which declares and defines space for the variable `ptr`, which will be used as a pointer. Within the program, somewhere

```
var1 = 2;
```

initializes the value of `var1` to 2, and

```
ptr = &var1;
```

places the address of `var1` into the pointer so that

```
*ptr == 2
```

Another use of & is to pass the address of a variable as a function parameter where the function needs to change a variable's value. (Remember that functions only get passed copies of their parameters and therefore don't have direct access to them.) In this way functions can be passed a location to change, thus "indirectly" modifying a variable. The standard library function `scanf` requires this technique.

The unary `sizeof` operator has application when a programmer needs to know the size of a data type in order to perform some calculation or function based on the data type's size. This operator is a compile-time operator allowing the (possibly) machine-dependent nature of a data type's size to be considered if the program is moved to a different environment. A typical use of `sizeof` is to determine storage requirements for, and to allocate a space big enough to hold, a particular data structure. For example, the expression

```
alloc(sizeof(struct struct_name))
```

tells the compiler to generate a constant with a value of the size, in bytes, of the structure `struct_name` so that, at run time, the library function `alloc` can be passed the number of bytes of storage needed for it.[3]

The binary operators << and >> are used to shift the bits of the unsigned integer operand on the operators' left, to the left (<<) or right

---

[3]Note that the `sizeof` aggregate data type may be bigger than its pieces. This can result from padding that occurs to locate the data on an even address boundary.

(>>), respectively, by the positive integer value of the operand on the operators' right. Bits shifted out of the integer at the head are lost, and zeros are shifted in at the tail. (The head is defined by the direction of the shift.) Following is an example of these operations.

If opr1 is initialized to 16, and opr2 is initialized to 2, then for

opr1 << opr2

the result is 64, and for

opr1 >> opr2

the result is 4.

The single ternary (three-piece) operator exp1 ? exp2 : exp3 provides a convenient either/or capability based on a logical test on exp1, which allows the further evaluation of either exp2 or exp3. The ternary operator is used in places where one of two simple outcomes can be selected, based on a zero/nonzero logical test on another expression. The expression's outcomes must produce variables of the same type, or a zero and a pointer. (The latter option is allowed so that an invalid ptr value, a Ø, can be used as one outcome, with a valid pointer being the alternative.)

An example involving the use of a ternary operator is a statement that produces the clear-screen code for one of two different terminals. If you assume that the variable term_type is set to a value of zero (Ø) or one (1) elsewhere in a program, and that clr_code will later be sent to the terminal, then the expression

clr_code = term_type ? ADM3_CLR : ADDS_CLR;

will set clr_code to ADM3_CLR if term_type is nonzero; otherwise, clr_code is set to ADDS_CLR.

Assignment Operators

Another unique feature of C is its use of numeric and Boolean operators combined with assignment operators to produce a shortened form. This capability allows two elements to replace three.

The three statements

```
x = x + .1;
x = x / y;
x = x * 1.1;
```

represent a class of assignment operation that is common enough to warrant special attention. By letting the compiler know that the result of the expression is going to be assigned into one of the components of the expression, the compiler can possibly create more efficient machine instructions. The equivalent forms of the preceding examples are, respectively

```
x += .1;
x /= y;
x *= 1.1;
```

The general form for using assignment operators is

```
var1 op= var2;
```

where the op= is replaced by one of the following assignment operators:

```
 = assignment
+= addition
-= subtraction
*= multiplication
/= division
%= remainder
>>= shift right
<<= shift left
&= AND
^= XOR
|= OR
```

Although you may never have thought that a comma was an operator, in C a comma can be very important. It performs a sequencing role in expressions where one action needs to be performed before another, possibly to take advantage of (or avoid) side effects. Consider the example

```
while(c = getchar(), c != EOF)
    do something
```

in which the subexpressions are executed from left to right, with the results of all but the rightmost expression being ignored insofar as the test by while is concerned. What happens can be described by the expression

```
c = getchar()
```

which assigns the results of an invocation of the standard library routine getchar() (that merely returns the next character available from the keyboard) to the variable c. Then the comma tells the program to ignore this value (being nonzero, the value would result in a true evaluation) and to evaluate the subexpression

    c != EOF

which tests the character entered against the constant EOF. If c is not equal to EOF, the result of the subexpression is true, and something is done. Otherwise, when c is equal to EOF, the expression is evaluated as false, and the something is passed by.

Expressions, as well as the action statements they form, give a programmer the means to produce results from data that the program is given or creates. Flow control statements, discussed in the next chapter, provide the framework within which the programmer organizes the evaluation of expressions into functions.

4

Flow Control

The matter of *flow control* is vitally important even though it is included as the final topic in this discussion of the C programming language. When a programmer constructs programs with functions in C, those functions are controlled by using *flow control statements*.

The following three types of flow control statements are provided:

1. Conditional execution

2. Repeated execution

3. Interruption of execution

Flow control statements normally exercise their influence over a single action statement (an expression followed by a semicolon). This influence may be expanded to include as many action statements as needed by surrounding them with braces (just as in a function block). In the examples in each section of this chapter, you may safely replace a single action statement with multiple statements just by creating a statement block.

As with functions, with flow control statements the placement of braces (if required) and the statements themselves present an opportunity to advance or retard readability. Because C is a free-form language (meaning it doesn't see white space), C won't be offended by the inconsistent or illogical use of indenting and line spacing. Anyone, even the author himself, who later tries to read the code, however, may be easily confused. The style used in the examples is only a recommendation, and you may find equally valid forms in other code you examine. Consistency should be your most important concern.

Conditional Execution

The available *conditional execution* statements are the if and the switch. The if statement controls the action statements that follow it, based on a logical test of an expression. The switch statement controls its action statements based on an integer result from an expression that is compared to one or more constants for equality. As shown in table 4.1, the if statement has three forms.

Table 4.1
Forms of the if Statement

Form #1	Form #2	Form #3

`if(expression)`
`    statement`
	`if(expression)`
	`    statement`
	`else`
	`    statement`
		`if(expression)`
		`    statement`
		`else if(expression)`
		`    statement`
		`else if(expression)`
		`    statement`
		
		. . .
		
		`else`
		`    statement`

In form #1 the statement will be evaluated if the expression produces a nonzero (true) result. Multiple statements may be controlled if they are enclosed in braces. For example, in the code

```
if(var1 > 0) {
    var2 = var1 * 2;
    var3 = var1 / 2;
    var1--;
}
var4 = 250 / var2;
```

the use of braces controls the execution of three statements. The fourth statement is not controlled and will be executed regardless of the test on the logical expression in the if. To aid readability, you can indent the controlled statements to give a visual cue about what controls what.

Shown in form #2 is another alternative. This form can be used when there is a two-way decision to be made on the basis of a single logical test. Here the first statement (or statement block) is executed if the expression evaluates nonzero (true), and the second statement (or statement block) is executed if the expression is false. In the following example similar spacing and brace placement styles apply:

```
if(var1 > 0) {
     var2 = var1 * 2;
     var3 = var1 / 2;
     var1--;
}
else
     var4 = 250 / var2;
```

This modification of the example in form #1 allows the fourth statement to be reached only if the test expression is evaluated false. Note that because only a single statement is placed after the else, the statement is not surrounded by braces. Remember, however, that at least one statement must follow an if, even if that statement is a null statement (that is, ; by itself).

The if statement shown in form #3 is used when there are multiple paths over which control might flow, only one of which is to be performed based on a true test of the path's associated logical expression. Only the first statement block reached through a true test is executed. The final else, with no attached test expression, is a catchall that will allow control to pass to the else's statement block if the previous tests have all evaluated false. (This control statement is very similar to the switch except that the switch can only perform tests on int data types.)

The switch statement presents a simple-to-use and easy-to-read method for selecting among different statement blocks. The switch has the following form:

```
switch(expression) {
     case constant1:
          statement
          statement
     case constant2:
     case constant3:
          statement
          break;

     default:
          statement
          break;
}
```

The test expression for the switch produces an int that is compared with the constant expression placed after the keyword case and followed by a colon. (On the other hand, the if can compare any data type to produce a true/false result from the if's test expression.) The constants must have different values and are also required to be ints or character constants promotable to ints. The compiler will automatically promote char constants. (Here the distinction between constants and variables indicates that the value compared against must be known at compile time.)

When a match is found between the expression result and the constant following the case keyword, execution begins at the statement block associated with that constant through to the end of the switch or to the first break interruption statement (or return, continue, or goto), whichever comes first. At this point, control is passed to the first action or flow control statement after the closing brace of the switch. No braces are required to group statements between cases.

In the sample form shown above, the first case is followed by two statements, then more cases. If the test expression produces an integer that matches the constant attached to the first case, control flows through its statements, through the next cases, and finally stops at the break after the third case. Likewise, the second case defines an entry point that has an execution path identical to the third case. This case exists to allow more than one value of the test expression to reach a common set of statements. If the test expression matches the constant at the third case, only its single statement is executed before control is passed beyond the switch, because the flow is interrupted at the break.

The single, optional default entry point operates in a similar manner to the final else of the if in form #3. The default is a catchall that allows control to enter if no previous match is found. As already demonstrated, if there were no break statement above the default keyword, the program would happily march right on through the statement found under the default to the end of the switch.

The default keyword will typically be placed at the end of the other cases, but it doesn't need to be. This keyword just marks the place where execution will begin if no other match is found. In addition, the break is not required after the last case or default, but is recommended.

Repeated Execution

The available *repeated execution* statements are the while, do, and for. They provide for looping constructions in C. The while statement loops until its test expression becomes false, with the test being made at the start of each cycle. The do acts similarly, but the test is made at the end of each cycle. And the for is a composite of the while, an initialization step, and an iteration step. (BASIC programmers will notice for's likeness to the ubiquitous FOR-NEXT loop.) Forms of while and do are shown in table 4.2.

Table 4.2
Repeated Execution Statements

Form of the while Statement	Form of the do Statement

while(expression)
    statement
	do
	        statement
	    while(expression);

Form of the for Statement
for(init_expression; test_expression; iteration_expression)   statement

The while statement is probably the most commonly used control flow statement in C. The while allows some action to take place for as long as its test expression continues to produce a true result. The expression is evaluated before each cycle begins; therefore, an expression which is initially false (Ø) will avoid even the first execution of the statement block.

Like the if control statement, the while may influence as many statements as are included within braces to form a statement block. A style issue is also pertinent here because the placement of braces and indentation of controlled statements lend much to readability.

The statement

```
while(1) {
    var2 = var1 * 2;
    var3 = var1 / 2;
    var1--;
}
```

represents a common way to construct an endless loop that might be required to make a program repeat over and over again until it is aborted. (This subject will be discussed further in the section on interruption statements.)

The statement

```
while(var--) {
    var2 = var1 * 2;
    var3 = var1 / 2;
}
```

allows the expression to do some work (post-decrementing var) and at the same time to provide a value to be tested for deciding whether to continue executing the statement block.

The statement

```
while(!(inp(PORT) & 1))
    ;
```

is a more advanced but common way of saying that you want to do *nothing* while the value at PORT is not 1 (that is, while bit 0 is Ø). Remember that the earlier definition of an expression included functions. You should not be surprised, then, to find that this expression includes a function invocation.

In this statement did you notice the logical negation operator? It reverses the effect that would otherwise be obtained: loop while the value at PORT is equal to 1.

This expression also demonstrates the need for having at least one statement following a while, even if that statement is a null. (Such a statement is also needed with the if and, as you will see later, with the do and for.)

The do statement is most easily understood by contrasting it with the while. Whereas the while makes its logical test of the expression before anything happens, the do executes the statement block before testing the value of the expression. This approach can be used when some action must be undertaken first in order to get a value to test. Consider the loop

```
do {

    val1 = function(x , y);
    val2 = val1 * 2;

}while(val1);
```

in which the two statements are executed for as long as the value of val1 remains nonzero. Remember that negative numbers are nonzero, too. Notice also that no logical test (for example, >, <=, or ==) is required because the expression's value itself is enough to satisfy the requirements of a true/false test. When the value returned from the function is zero (Ø), this loop will end, and control will be passed to the next action or flow control statement after the do.

If there were only one statement, as in

```
do

    val = inp(PORT) & 1;

while(!val);
```

no braces would be required. At least one statement is required, however. Remember to include the final semicolon following the expression after the while.

The for statement combines three separate elements into one statement to improve readability by localizing the loop control action. The for statement is evaluated in the following three steps:

1. Initialize any variable(s)

2. Perform any logical test(s)

> If true,
> perform the statement(s)
> If false,
> exit the loop

3. Evaluate any iteration expressions

The for may be replaced with one or more assignment statements and one while statement, as shown in the following comparison:

1. Written as a `for` statement

```
for(var1=0; var1 < 10; var1++)
     var2 += var1;
```

2. Written as an assignment and a `while`

```
var1 = 0;
while(var < 10) {
     var2 += var1;
     var1++;
}
```

Notice here the reliance on indentation to help identify which statements are in the loop. The other flow control statements use indentation in the same way. Such a technique becomes even more desirable when there are many possibly nested controlled statements.

```
for(var1 = 0, var2 = 0; (var1 < var2) && (var2 != 0); var1++) {
     var3 = var1 / var2;
     var2 *= LIMIT * var1 + func(var1);
}
```

This example shows how more than one initialization can be performed by separating the expressions with a comma. The iteration field of the `for` can likewise contain several independent expressions separated by commas. (Any number of expressions are possible, but using many makes the statement more difficult to read.) A compound logical expression is used here to allow the loop to continue or stop based on a more complicated test. Generally, the best use of these expressions includes only those variables directly connected with the iteration involved.

The initialization expression can do more than set a variable to zero. And the iteration expression can be more complex than a simple increment or decrement. Either can be any legal expression. The variable(s) used in the iteration expression can be affected elsewhere in the statement block. In addition, elements of the `for` statement can be omitted, as in

```
for(;;)
     func();
```

which is the same as a `while(1)` because either will loop forever (resulting from the absence of the middle logical test that defaults to true). Obviously, this statement has no initialization or iteration expressions to worry about.

Interruption of Execution

Four *flow interruption* statements are available: `break`, `continue`, `goto`, and `return`. They provide the ability to stop doing something that was started by the foregoing repeated execution statements. Following are the four forms for these interruption statements:

```
break;

continue;

goto label;
label:

return;
```

The `break` statement was introduced with the discussion of the `switch`. The `break` interrupted the flow of the program at the completion of the statements associated with a particular `case`. (`break` passed control to the end of the `switch`.) The `break` can also be used with the repeated execution statements (`for`, `while`, and `do`) where `break` has the same effect. Following is an example showing how a `break` might be used in a `while`:

```
while(var1--) {
    if(var2 == 20)
        break;
    var1 += var2;
}
var2 = var;
```

If the variable `var2` is equal to 20, the `break` statement interrupts the `while` and passes control to the assignment following the closing brace of the statement block.

Wherever the `break` is used, the innermost loop in which `break` is found is terminated. This interruption statement can be used when repeated execution statements are built inside one another, as demonstrated by the following:

```
for(var1 = 0; var1 < 20; var1++) {
    while(var2 = func()) {
        if(!(var1 % var2))
            break;
    }
}
```

The outer loop incrementing var1 from 0 to 19 controls an inner loop that assigns the results of a function call to var2. The inner loop stops when the value returned from func() is zero *or* when the remainder from the division of var1 by var2 is zero. Control is then passed out of the while and back to the for. (Notice that the braces in this example are optional; each test expression controls only one statement. Notice also that the break, located within the control of an if, had its loop-terminating effect on the while.)

Use of the continue statement follows the same pattern as that of break. With continue, however, control is not passed outside the loop. Control flows to the end of the statement block where the test expression is immediately reevaluated. (In the case of the for, control flows through the iteration expression, then to the test expression.) The continue is used to bypass all the rest of the action statements between continue and the end of the statement block:

```
do {
     var1 = PI / 180 * radius;
     var2 = func(var1);

     if(var2 == 0)
          continue;

     var3 = var1 / var2;

}while(var3 > 1);
```

The value assigned to var3 is the quotient of the division of var1 by var2. Because you wouldn't want to divide var1 by zero, this program fragment uses a continue after the test to find out whether var2 is zero. If the test is true, the continue will pass control to the while part of the do statement where the loop test expression is evaluated.

Fanatic believers in structured programming will never use a goto, but it does have a place in C. A goto can be very useful in complicated constructions that suddenly have to deal with an error condition. Such constructions can use a goto to get to an error-processing routine, safely jumping out of nested dos, fors, or whiles.

Another legitimate use of goto is to allow common blocks of code to be reached from different places, thereby reducing duplication or the need to invoke a function. The following switch is used in the `scan` function in Part III; the expression has been edited to re-move some detail that isn't relevant to this example.

```
switch(data_type[n]) {
    case 'd' :
        if(right_flag[n])
            temp = strlen(entry_chars[n])
        else
            temp = 0;
        goto move_it;

    case 'f' :
        temp = strlen(entry_chars[n]) - strlen(work_space);
        goto move_it;

    case 's' :
        if(right_flag[n])
            temp = strlen(entry_chars[n]) - strlen(work_space);
        else
            temp = 0;
    move_it:
        while(c = *work_space++)
            entry_chars[n][temp++] = c;
        reprint(n);
        break;

    default:
        break;
}
```

As shown here, the `goto` is used by placing a `goto` statement where needed (you can have several `goto`s) and a `label` statement (you can have only one for each identifier) at the destination point. An important note to remember is that the scope of a `goto` is within the current function block. (You cannot use a `goto` to reach a label in another function, but you may use the `setjmp()`/`longjmp()` functions, which are part of the standard library.)

Finally, the `return` statement has the following forms, each with a different purpose:

```
return;
```

```
return expression;
```

The first form is used strictly to interrupt the flow within a function and to return, without a value, to the parent function. Some problems may arise if the invoking function tries to make some use of the value that wasn't returned! The `return` statement has legitimate use, however, when a function manipulates some external data, simply waits for some event to occur, or just doesn't have anything to say. (The function might be declared `void` in this case; see the section on declarations in Chapter 0.)

More frequently, when a function returns some value, the second form is used, as in

```
return var1;
```

The returned value can be a status (true/false) to report that the function was able to perform its task, or a value of the type that the function was declared to return. (A common source of errors is a function attempting to return a value of a type different from that for which the function was declared. A forced assignment is created, and data may be lost or misinterpreted. See the section on conversion rules in Chapter 1.)

The `return` statement can also be a place where some work gets done, for its attached expression may include any legal combination of variables, function calls, and operators.

Following is a perfectly legal way to create a simple function that just doubles its input parameter:

```
double twice(var1)
double var1;
{
    return var1 * 2;
}
```

Note that the function is declared to return a `double`; the `return` therefore sends back a value of that type.

Conclusion

What else is there to learn about C? Many books contain more pages than these to cover more material. This book's instruction does not end here, however. Part III is devoted to helping you uncover the secrets of C by enabling you to become a participant instead of a bystander. This last section starts with some simple programs you can type into your computer, compile, link, and watch. These programs have many comments and are preceded by explanations for reference if you get stuck. They use only the standard library functions so you can get used to C without worrying about writing your own functions.

Next are introduced some reasonably complex functions that you can enter into your own function library. You will soon be designing and writing the programs that use these functions. They demonstrate more advanced coding techniques and emphasize generality of purpose.

Finally, more complex functions are combined into complete programs that use other functions developed in previous sections, as well as functions from the standard library. These functions are immediately useful in their own right and also provide experience in creating programs from several modules.

Remember that it's next to impossible to damage your computer by writing programs that don't work, so don't be afraid of making mistakes as you learn C. Learning C can be great fun. Who knows, maybe someday you'll write a book!

Part III
Introduction to the Functions

Many competing design philosophies are at work in the following functions. Before you begin to examine the functions, here is a brief description of them and their priorities.

Common C Functions is intended to give the newcomer to C some functions to enter into a computer and get working on in as short a time as possible. One advantage of C functions, however, is that they can be collected into libraries and used later, possibly under different circumstances. To realize fully this advantage requires designing functions with a high degree of generality. And sometimes generality can be obtained only at the cost of simplicity. By separating the working part of a function from the output-producing portion, you can produce a rather general function with little immediate benefit.

In most of these functions, the purpose is to demonstrate generality in function design. Thus, the newcomer will be taken directly into battle with some of the more complex issues in C, but presumably with the side benefit of a deeper understanding. These design features are clearly described. When a function's generality obscures your ability to get something out of the function, a minimal surrounding program has been provided to access and produce results from the function. Typically, such an approach involves requesting input from the user, passing it to the function, and displaying the results on the console.

Many documentation styles in C functions are also available. For consistency, I have followed my own advice in earlier chapters and included a standard header and line-by-line comments. Though the comments are generous, they are included primarily to reveal the logical flow of the program and to describe local oddities, rather than to interpret the adjacent program lines.

In one way or another, most of these functions rely on other functions defined elsewhere. The purpose of the subordinate function is described thoroughly enough so that you won't need to be constantly flipping all over to trace execution. In the index, the functions are listed alphabetically and highlighted in a special font to aid the diehards who believe that the index is the only true path to enlightenment. Likewise, all constant values are represented with capitalized identifiers to promote the use of `#defines` when you are dealing with values that have some intrinsic meaning to the function.

Finally, I know that the concept of a "standard C library" is a figment of the unleashed imagination. But instead of writing and describing every function used here, which is (or should be) a part of such a standard library, I have provided a list of these functions in Appendix C, together with their argument lists, variable types, and brief descriptions. You should first confirm that the operation of my standard library is the same as yours to be sure that our results will be the same.

Good luck!

Function Group One: Introductory Functions

module:	functions:
saygetmv. c	void say() void get() void move()

module:	functions:
atoi. c	int _atoi() char *_itoa() char *itoa() char *ltoa() long atol() int atoi() char *lmod()

module:	function:
calc. c	main()

module:	functions:
keepme. c	int keep_me() main() for demo

module:	functions:
listme. c	int listme() main() for demo

modules:	function:
macros. h macros. c	main() for demo

The functions in this group lay a foundation for those that follow. The emphasis here is on the construction of modules, use of various data types, simple flow control and action statements, basic I/O functions, and the creation of a program from several pieces. This group marks a transition between the first five chapters, which were descriptive and tutorial in nature, and the functions that make up the balance of the text. After this group of simple, limited-purpose functions, we will explore some useful ones that will give you a real taste of C.

saygetmv.c

The three functions included in this module are used with the calc. c program. In the standard library, these functions have more powerful equivalents that would normally be used, but the functions are presented here as simple alternatives that can be easily understood by the novice. The functions included and their standard library equivalents are the following:

To move a string of chars from one place to another:

move(dst, src) — strcpy(dst, src)	Moves characters until the end of string null is found, then finally moves null
strncpy(dst, src, n)	Moves n characters only

To print a string of characters:

say(ptr) — puts(ptr)	Prints a string on stdout until null is found and then adds a newline
printf(ptr)	Powerful string-formatting function that can include numeric-string conversions; directs output to stdout
fputs(fp, ptr)	Similar to puts except that output is directed to the stream defined by the file pointer fp
fprintf(fp, ptr)	Similar to printf except that output is directed to the stream defined by fp
write(fp, ptr, n)	Writes n characters from the location ptr to the stream defined by fp

To retrieve a string of characters:

get(ptr) — gets(ptr) Gets a character string
from stdin and places
the string at ptr

fgets(ptr, n, fp) Gets n characters from
the input stream defined
by fp and places them at
ptr followed by a null

read(fp, ptr, n) Gets n characters from
the stream defined by fp
and places them at ptr

The concept of I/O streams is simple, yet it can be confusing to the novice. What is meant by a "stream" is a flow of characters (or bytes) into or out of a program. This stream can flow through a variety of devices. Ideally, the device chosen should be insignificant to the operation of the program. Furthermore, because the stream is selected by means of a pointer variable (in the preceding examples, fp is a pointer to a structure giving the details about a particular stream), another stream can be selected simply by changing the location where the pointer points.

saygetmv.c

```
/*  module title: saygetmv.c
 *  function names: void say(), void get(), void move()
 *
 *  author: Kim J. Brand
 *
 *  revision history:
 *    version/--date--/by reason---------------------------------------------
 *      1.0   10/01/84 kb Common C Functions initial release
 *
 *  compiled with: stdio.h
 *  compiled by:
 *
 *  linked with: calc.c
 *  linked by:
 *
 *  problems:
 *
 *  description: simple input, output, and string (memory) move functions
 *
 */
```

```c
#include <stdio.h>

void move(dst, src)     /* moves the characters pointed to by src    */
char *dst;              /*  to where the destination pointer points  */
char *src;
{
        do
            *dst++ = *src;      /* a way that does not require an     */
        while (*src++);         /*  intermediate character variable; */
                                /*  note: also moves the null if the */
                                /*  source string is of zero length  */
/*
 *      char c;
 *
 *      while (c=*src++)        this way, although equivalent, is
 *          *dst++ = c;         less efficient
 *      *dst = c;
 */

}

void say(ptr)           /* prints string pointed to by pointer, on the */
char *ptr;              /*  stdout device, usually the console         */
{
        char c;

        while (c = *ptr++)      /* all strings in C end with a null; in this */
            putchar(c);         /*  case, that's what stops the music        */

}

void get(ptr)                   /* simple function to get a string of chars  */
char *ptr;                      /*  from stdin (usually the console) and put */
{                               /*  them at the address passed               */

        char c;                 /* all-purpose character variable            */

        while ((c = getchar()) != '\n') /* keep getting characters until */
            *ptr++ = c;                  /*  a newline is reached         */

        *ptr = '\0';                     /* remember to place the null    */

}
```

atoi.c

This module contains the source code for several of the most popular ASCII-to-integer and integer-to-ASCII conversion functions. Two simple functions whose names begin with an underscore [_atoi() and _itoa()] are included solely to serve the limited purposes required by the calc. c program. These functions may be studied and quickly understood within that context.

The remaining functions in this module are similar to the "real" functions that may be supplied with your standard library. They incorporate more complex coding techniques and offer greater versatility. The functions are these:

long atol(str)	convert an ASCII string into a long
int atoi(str)	convert an ASCII string into an int
char *ltoa(str, val)	convert a long value into an ASCII string at str
char *itoa(str, val)	convert an int value into an ASCII string at str

The functions that produce strings from values make use of a function named lmod which uses recursion to convert numeric arguments "from the inside out." Both functions that convert integer arguments are really just "fronts" for calls to their long cousins. This convenience allows the programmer to be less concerned about the type of arguments required by a particular function. Although it is possible to get along with only the long versions of both these conversion functions, at some time int values will predictably be passed to, or assumed to be returned from, the long functions, thereby causing undesirable results.

atoi.c

```
/*  module title: atoi.c
 *  function names: int _atoi(), atoi()
 *                  long atol()
 *                  char *itoa(), *lmod(), *ltoa()
 *                  void _itoa()
 *
 *  author: Kim J. Brand
 *
 *  revision history:
 *      version/--date--/by reason-----------------------------------------
 *        1.0   10/01/84 kb Common C Functions initial release
 *
 *  compiled with: stdio.h, ctype.h
 *  compiled by:
 *
 *  linked with: calc()
 *  linked by:
 *
 *  problems: none known
 *
 *  description: The functions starting with underscores are simplified
 *               ascii-to-integer and integer-to-ascii functions used in the
 *               calc() program; those following are more complete versions
 *               normally available in the standard library. They are based
 *               on functions supplied with the Ecosoft C Compiler.
 *
 *               Depending on the compiler, you may need to #include the
 *               character type macros. (For example, Lattice requires
 *               <ctype.h>.)
 *
 *               The itoa(), ftoa(), dtoa() functions also may be accomplished
 *               by using sprintf() instead.
 *
 */

#include <stdio.h>
#include <ctype.h>

int _atoi(ptr)              /* ascii-to-integer conversion function   */
char *ptr;                  /*  named with leading _ to avoid confusion */
{                           /*  with real library function atoi        */

     char c;
     int result = 0;                   /* initialize result to zero */
     int sign = 1;                     /* makes assumption that     */
                                       /*  number is positive       */
     if (*ptr == '-') {
          sign = -1;                   /* set sign to -1 if first   */
          ptr++;                       /*  character is minus sign  */
     }
```

```
                                              /* as we get a character out */
        while (c = *ptr++) {                  /*  of string, we are also   */
                                              /*  testing character for    */
                                              /*  being true, nonzero      */

            if (c < '0' || c > '9')           /* check to make sure that   */
                continue;                     /*  digit is in range        */

            result = result * 10 + (c - '0'); /* multiply (shift left)     */
                                              /*  current result by one    */
        }                                     /*  power of ten as we add   */
                                              /*  new digit                */

        return (result * sign);               /* when string ends,         */
                                              /*  return the result        */
}


void _itoa(ptr, n)              /* convert integer n to ascii string where */
char *ptr;                      /*  ptr points; must have enough room       */
int n;
{
        int i;                          /* all-purpose counter             */
        static int decade[] = {         /* array of powers of ten indexed  */
                10000,                  /*  in reverse order               */
                1000,
                100,
                10,
                1
        };
        char c;                         /* string character being worked on */

        if (n < 0) {                    /* make n positive and place a dash */
            n *= -1;                    /*  in front of string if began as  */
            *ptr++ = '-';               /*  negative number                 */
        }                               /* increment pointer after placing  */
                                        /*  minus sign                      */

        n++;                            /* needed because program does not  */
                                        /*  go all the way down to 10**0    */
                                        /*  that is, biased by 1            */

        for (i = 0; i < 5; i++) {       /* function can handle only         */
                                        /*  numbers in the range            */
            c = '0';                    /*  -32768 <= n <= 32767, 5 digits  */

            do {                        /* fill this position with current  */
                *ptr = c++;             /*  assumption of value             */
            }
```

```
            while ((n -= decade[i]) > 0);  /* will be right when this is neg  */

            n += decade[i];                /* then correct for too many       */
            ptr++;                         /* subtractions and bump pointer    */

        }

        *ptr = '\0';                       /* append null                      */
}


long atol(str)                /* here again, the more general case of   */
                              /* converting a long is covered so that   */
char *str;                    /* converting an int can be a subset      */
{
    long value = 0;                        /* a working variable                */
    int sign = 1;                          /* a place to keep track of the sign */

    if (*str == '\t' || *str == ' ')
        str++;

    if(isdigit(*str) && *str!='0' || (*str=='-' || *str=='+') && str[1]!='0' ) {
                              /* handle decimal number cases first      */
        if(*str == '-') {     /* determine if there's a leading sign and */
            ++str;            /*   move string pointer past it           */
            sign = -1;        /* adjust sign flag accordingly, this is   */
        }                     /*   used for decimal numbers only         */
        else {
            if(*str == '+')
                str++;
        }

        while(isdigit(*str))
            value = value * 10 + *str++ - '0';  /* accumulate it         */
    }

    else if(tolower(str[1])=='x') {        /* handle hex values here      */

        while(isdigit(*str) || (tolower(*str)>='a' && tolower(*str)<='f')) {

            value *= 16;                   /* hex decades come in powers of 16 */

            if(isdigit(*str))
                value += *str++ -'0';
            else
                value += tolower(*str++) - 'a' + 10;
        }
    }
    else if(isdigit(str[1])) {             /* handle octal values here    */
```

```
        while(isdigit(*str)) {
            value<<=3;                      /* octal digits come in powers of  */
                                            /* eight; multiplying by eight is  */
            value+=*str++ - '0';            /* same as shifting left by 3      */
        }
    }
    return (sign * value);                  /* if none of the conversion specs */
}                                           /* work, just return a zero; note  */
                                            /* that this is a long zero        */

int atoi(str)                               /* finally the funtion we're       */
char *str;                                  /* interested in                   */
{
    return (atol(str));             /* and again, notice the cast from an int  */
}                                   /* to a long before invoking atol          */



char *lmod(str, arg, modn)                  /* this function is called by ltoa */
                                            /* to convert a numeric value arg  */
char *str;                                  /* in base modn into a string at   */
long arg;                                   /* str; notice that it is recursive*/
int modn;
{
    long    temp2;
    int     temp1;

    temp1 = arg % modn;
    temp2 = arg / modn;
    if(temp2)
        str=lmod(str, temp2, modn);
    *str++ = (temp1 > 9) ? (temp1 + 'a' - 10) : (temp1 + '0');
    return (str);
}

char *ltoa(str, arg)                        /* this function is included because */
                                            /* the more general case of convert-*/
char *str;                                  /* ing a long to an ascii string    */
long arg;                                   /* satisfies that for converting an */
                                            /* int                              */
{

    char *rtn=str;

    if(arg < 0) {                           /* if value is less than zero, just */
        arg = -arg;                         /* flip its sign                    */
        *str++ = '-';                       /* and prepend a minus sign         */
        if(arg < 0) {
            strcpy(str, "2147483648");      /* still negative means it's */
            return (rtn);                   /* too big a number to be     */
        }                                   /* signed, so give it all     */
    }                                       /* we got                     */
```

111

```
        str = lmod(str,arg,10);
        *str = '\0';                    /* tack on a null            */
        return (rtn);
}

char *itoa(str,arg)            /* the actual function that would be called  */
                              /*  to convert an integer function into an  */
char *str;                    /*  ascii string at str                     */
int arg;
{
        return (ltoa(str,(long)arg));  /* note its integer argument is cast */
                                       /*  to a long before being passed to */
                                       /*  ltoa                             */
}
```

calc.c

This simple program demonstrates several C concepts, most notably the ability of a C program to make use of functions compiled separately in different modules. The program implements a rudimentary, four-function integer calculator that receives input and writes output solely to the user console.

A maximum of six five-digit numbers may be entered after the ":" prompt. A return is entered in response to the ":" prompt after all the numbers have been entered. Afterward, the program provides a "?" prompt for the operator. At this point a "+", "-", "/", or "*" may be supplied. The program calculates the answer and prints it on the next line after an equal sign. If bad data is entered, the program responds with " what??" and prints "=BAD DATA" where the answer would go.

Sample execution:

```
COMMON C FUNCTIONS
4 FUNCTION CALCULATOR

:4
:4
:
?*
=00016

:5
:20
:13
:
?+
00038

:50
:3
:
?(  what??
=BAD DATA
```

calc.c

```
/*   module title: calc.c
 *   function name: main() for demo
 *
 *   author: Kim J. Brand
 *
 *   revision history:
 *      version/--date--/by reason-----------------------------------------
 *         1.0   10/01/84 kb Common C Functions initial release
 *
 *   compiled with: stdio.h
 *   compiled by:
 *
 *   linked with: void _atoi(), _itoa(), get(), move(), say()
 *   linked by:
 *
 *   problems:
 *
 *   description: a four-function integer calculator to demonstrate the use
 *                of console input/output and ascii-integer-ascii conversion
 */


#include <stdio.h>

main()                                  /* this is the whole program      */
{
        int c;                          /* a character holder that can take */
                                        /*  on the value of EOF (-1)      */
        int n;                          /* all-purpose counters           */
        int i;
        int number[6];                  /* space for 6 numbers plus       */
        int answer;                     /*  an answer                     */
        char string[6][10];
        char result[10];                /* numbers represented as ascii   */
                                        /*  character strings, 6 each of 8+1 */
                                        /*  characters long; 1 is for     */
                                        /*  the null; result is the answer */


        void say();
        void get();
        void move();
        void _itoa();
        int _atoi();

        say("\nCOMMON C FUNCTIONS");              /* a little vanity       */
        say("\n4 FUNCTION CALCULATOR\n");
```

```
for (;;) {                              /* this means forever         */

    answer = 0;                         /* initialize answer to zero */
                                        /*  every time through loop  */
    for (n = 0; n < 6; n++) {
        putchar(' :' );                 /* tells user when new        */
                                        /*  numbers are expected     */

        get(string[n]);                 /* returns ascii version      */
                                        /*  of the number             */
                                        /* an entry with a null       */

        if (string[n][0] == 0)          /* a null first character     */
            break;                      /*  signals the person is     */
                                        /*  done entering numbers     */
    }

    for (i = 0; i < n; i++)             /* for number of strings      */
        number[i] = _atoi(string[i]);   /* note that atoi gets the    */
                                        /*  address of the string     */

    putchar(' ?' );                     /* tells user to enter        */
                                        /*  an operator               */

    switch (c = getchar()) {

        case '*' :                      /* multiply                   */
            answer = number[0] * number[1];
            _itoa(result, answer);
            break;

        case '-' :                      /* subtract                   */
            answer = number[0] - number[1];
            _itoa(result, answer);
            break;

        case '+' :                      /* add                        */
            for (i = 0; i < n; i++)
                answer += number[i];
            _itoa(result, answer);
            break;

        case '/' :                      /* divide                     */
            answer = number[0] / number[1];
            _itoa(result, answer);
            break;
```

```
        case EOF:
            exit(0);                          /* the way you leave          */

        default:                              /* anything else              */
            move(result, "BAD DATA");
            break;
    }

    putchar('=');                             /* only ascii strings may be */
    say(result);                              /*  passed to say()           */
    say("\n\n");                              /*  one at a time             */

  }
}
```

keepme.c

This almost trivial program is intended to demystify the creation of disk files in a C program. As you will notice, there are three parts to file manipulation:

1. Opening the file
2. Putting something in it
3. Closing the file

Opening a file is usually accomplished by the fopen() function. Files may be opened in a variety of ways to suit many purposes. You'll have to check your compiler documentation to find out what ways are supported. Generally, methods are available to open a file for reading or writing, or both. And for each method, you'll have to decide if the file will hold ASCII or binary data.

The primary distinction here is in the handling of special characters, such as the newline (\n) and EOF (-1 or Øx1a). For ASCII files that keepme() deals with, we'll want to take advantage of the automatic conversion of newlines into carriage-return/line-feed pairs, which the "w" format offers. The fopen() function returns a pointer to a structure; we assign this pointer to the suitably declared variable fp.

Putting something in the file is as easy as it can be. The putc() function includes one parameter for the file pointer variable and one for the character we want to store. Many other functions use the same technique. Among them are fprintf() and fputs().

Every file that gets opened must also get closed so that the buffers which are created get written to disk. Closing the file is performed by the fclose() function. Its only argument is the same file pointer we received from fopen.

Sample execution (under MS-DOS):

```
A>keepme file

Keeping characters in file.
Enter your message here:
hello world
^Z

13 characters kept

A>
```

keepme.c

```
/*  module title: keepme.c
 *  function name: int keep_me()
 *                  main() for demo
 *
 *  author: Kim J. Brand
 *
 *  revision history:
 *     version/--date--/by reason------------------------------------------
 *        1.0   10/01/84 kb Common C Functions initial release
 *
 *  compiled with: stdio.h, ctype.h
 *  compiled by:
 *
 *  linked with:
 *  linked by:
 *
 *  problems:
 *
 *  description: demonstration function to introduce file I/O
 *                  and handle command line arguments
 *
 */

#include <stdio.h>
#include <ctype.h>

                               /* demonstration main()                   */

main(argc,argv)                /* take one parameter from command line:  */
int argc;                      /* copy console characters to file specified */
char *argv[];                  /* on command line                        */
{
        int count;             /* so can report number of characters saved */
        int keep_me();

        if (argc != 2) {                              /* report incorrect */
            puts("keepme: usage: keepme filename");   /* invocation       */
            exit(1);
        }

        count = keep_me(argv[1]);           /* tells keep_me to use this */
                                            /* file name to store data   */
        printf("\n%d characters kept\n", count);
}
```

```
int keep_me(name)                    /* passed a pointer to character string as  */
char *name;                          /*  file name to copy stdin keystrokes to;  */
{                                    /*  returns characters stored               */

        int c;                       /* all-purpose character variable           */
        int count = 0;               /* returns the count of chars               */
                                     /*  stored; start at 0                      */
        FILE *fp;                    /* a pointer to data of type FILE           */
                                     /*  a cleverly disguised structure          */
                                     /*  defined in stdio.h                      */
        FILE *fopen();

        fp = fopen(name, "w");       /* open file                                */

        if (!fp)                     /* NULL return means trouble;               */
                                     /*  say so and return count = 0             */
            printf("\nCan't open %s, returning to DOS",name);

        else {
            printf("\nKeeping characters in %s.", name);
            puts("\nEnter your message here:");

            while ((c = getchar()) != EOF) {    /* stops at EOF, see stdio.h */
                                                /*  usually ctrl-Z or D      */
                if (!isprint(c) && c != '\n')   /* do not store unprintable  */
                    continue;                   /*  characters, except \n    */
                putc(c, fp);                    /*  puts them in file        */
                count++;                        /*  and increments count     */
                if (c == '\n')
                    count++;                    /* putc in the w mode makes  */
                                                /*  two characters out \n    */
            }                                   /*  a cr/lf pair is stored   */
        }

        fclose(fp);                  /* must close file or all                   */
                                     /*  is lost                                 */
        return (count);              /* return number saved                      */
}
```

listme.c

This program performs the reverse function of the keepme.c program. listme.c will copy (to the console, the printer, or another file) the contents of a file. The point demonstrated here is that file I/O in C can be quite flexible and still be easy to perform.

The command line for listme.c under MS-DOS might look something like this:

```
A>listme file
```

Because there are only two command line arguments, the output will automatically be sent to the console. If, on the other hand, the command line were

```
A>listme file prn:
```

the contents of file would be sent to the printer. Finally, if you entered

```
A>listme file file1
```

the first file would be copied to the file file1.

If the console is the destination file, listme will pause after every 23 lines and print the prompt RETURN. Any character typed will cause the RETURN message to be removed and the next 23 lines to be displayed. After the listing is finished, the number of characters read or written will be reported to stdout.

Sample execution (using the same file saved in the keepme example):

```
A>listme file
hello world

13 characters listed

A>
```

listme.c

```
/*  module title: listme.c
 *  function name: int list_me()
 *                 main() for demo
 *
 *  author: Kim J. Brand
 *
 *  revision history:
 *     version/--date--/by reason-------------------------------------------
 *        1.0   10/01/84 kb Common C Functions initial release
 *
 *  compiled with: stdio.h
 *  compiled by:
 *
 *  linked with: int inchar()
 *  linked by:
 *
 *  problems: none known
 *
 *  description: simple file-listing utility to demonstrate file I/O and
 *               redirection effects; if the destination is stdout (the
 *               console), the function pauses after each screenful to wait
 *               for user input; returns # of characters listed
 */

#include <stdio.h>

#define PAGE 23

main(argc,argv)         /* simple main included for demonstration       */
int argc;               /*  purposes only; tell listme() which file to open */
char *argv[];           /*  and where to send output                    */
{
        int count;

        int listme();

        if (argc < 2 || argc > 3) {
            puts("\nlistme: usage: listme src [dst]");
            exit(1);
        }

        /* if only two arguments passed, give a null string as second  */
        /* to listme(); otherwise, pass name of output file            */

        count = listme(argv[1], (argc < 3) ? "" : argv[2]);

        printf("\n%d characters listed", count);

}
```

121

```
int listme(src, dst)              /* open src file and send to destination  */
char *src;                        /*  file; the parameters are file names   */
char *dst;                        /* dst is null if stdout is desired: console */
{
        int c;                    /* all-purpose character variable,        */
        int count = 0;            /*  returns the number of characters      */
                                  /*  processed                             */
        int line = 0;             /* keeps track of number of lines sent    */

        FILE *fp_src;
        FILE *fp_dst;             /* pair of pointers to structures of      */
                                  /*  FILE type                             */

        FILE *fopen();
        int inchar();


        if (!(fp_src = fopen(src, "r"))) {    /* much done here:            */
            printf("\nCan't open %s.", src);  /* open file if error; that   */
            return (count);                   /*  is, if pointer returned   */
        }                                     /*  is null, return           */
                                              /*  after printing message    */
        if (strlen(dst) == 0)
            fp_dst = stdout;                  /* way to get to              */
        else                                  /*  console indirectly        */
            fp_dst = fopen(dst, "w");         /*  unless a file name is      */
                                              /*  used                       */

        if (!fp_dst)                          /* make same check on          */
            printf("\nCan't open %s.", dst);  /*  output file as on          */
                                              /*  input file; error falls    */
                                              /*  through to fclose below    */
        else {
            while ((c = getc(fp_src)) != EOF) { /* if all well, copy input   */
                count++;                      /*  to output while there is   */
                putc(c, fp_dst);              /*  more left                  */
                if (c == '\n') {
                    count++;                  /* because each \n             */
                    line++;                   /*  really represents \n\r     */
                    if (fp_dst == stdout) {   /*  on output                  */
                        if (!(line % PAGE)) { /* at each page, if stdout,    */
                            fprintf(fp_dst, "RETURN");
                            fflush(fp_dst);   /* ensure RETURN is written    */
                                              /*  to console                 */
                            inchar();         /*  pause for input            */
                            fprintf(fp_dst, "\b\b\b\b\b\b      \b\b\b\b\b\b");
                            fflush(fp_dst);
                        }
                    }
                }
            }
        }
}
```

```
    fclose(fp_src);                    /* be sure to clean up   */

    if (fp_dst != stdout)              /* do not close stdout   */
        fclose(fp_dst);

    return (count);
}
```

macros.c

This program demonstrates the use of parameterized macros. It includes the macros. h file so that the several conversions are accomplished with in-line macro expansion rather than function calls. If execution speed is to be optimized, this method is preferred, but it usually has the effect of making a program larger.

Sample execution:

```
x = 123.450000
x = 12345
x = 12345
x = 678.900000
x = 67890
x = 2354
x = 123.450000
x = 12345
x = 123
x = 0.450000
x = 5.080000
x = 0.787402
x = 0.261799
x = 89.381416
x = 49.611665
x = 0.987672
x = 12.25
x = 12.30
x = 471.435248
x = 15.187500
x = 4.616100
```

macros.h

```
/* MACROS include file from
 *
 * COMMON C FUNCTIONS
 *
 * here are several conversion macros to be used in place of functions
 * where appropriate
 *
 * double _PI                      the value of pi to 14 places
 * double _E                       the value of e to 14 places
 *
 * int/unsigned/long INT(x)        produces the integer portion of the variable
 * float/double FRAC(x)            produces the fractional part of the variable
 * ABS(x)                          produces the absolute value of the variable
 * MIN(x,y)                        produces the lesser of x or y
 * MAX(x,y)                        produces the greater of x or y
 *
 * double INCH_CM(x)               converts inch argument to centimeters
 * double CM_INCH(x)               converts cm argument to inches
 * double DEG_RAD(x)               converts degrees argument to radians
 * double RAD_DEG(x)               converts radians argument to degrees
 * double OZ_GRMS(x)               converts ounces argument to grams
 * double GRMS_OZ(x)               converts grams argument to ounces
 * double HRS_DHRS(x)              converts hrs.min to hours and decimal parts
 * double DHRS_HRS(x)              converts hours with decimal parts to hours.min
 * double RCTNGL_AREA(x,y)         produces area of rectangle given side1, side2
 *                                     arguments
 * double CRCL_AREA(x)             produces area of circle from radius argument
 * double RTRNGL_AREA(x,y)         produces area of right triangle from base,
 *                                     height arguments
 *
 */

#define _PI 3.141592653589793
#define _E 2.718281828459045

#define INT(x) ((int)(x))
#define FRAC(x) ((x)-(int)(x))
#define ABS(x)   (((x)<0) ? -(x) : (x))
#define MIN(x,y) (((x)<(y)) ? (x) : (y))
#define MAX(x,y) (((x)<(y)) ? (y) : (x))

#define INCH_CM(x) ((x)*2.54)
#define CM_INCH(x) ((x)*0.393701)
#define DEG_RAD(x) ((x)*0.017453293)
#define RAD_DEG(x) ((x)*57.29577951)
#define OZ_GRMS(x) ((x)*28.349523)
#define GRMS_OZ(x) ((x)*0.035274)
#define HRS_DHRS(x) ((int)(x)+((x)-(int)(x))/0.60)
#define DHRS_HRS(x) ((int)(x)+((x)-(int)(x))*0.60)
#define CRCL_AREA(x) ((x)*(x)*_PI)
#define RCTNGL_AREA(x,y) ((x)*(y))
#define TRNGL_AREA(x,y) ((x)*(y)*0.5)
```

macros.c

```
/*  module title: macros.c
 *  function names: main() for demo
 *
 *  author: Kim J. Brand
 *
 *  revision history:
 *     version/--date--/by reason-------------------------------------------
 *        1.0   10/01/84 kb Common C Functions initial release
 *
 *  compiled with: stdio.h macros.h
 *  compiled by:
 *
 *  linked with:
 *  linked by:
 *
 *  problems:
 *
 *  description: a demo program for the macros brought in from the macros.h
 *               include file
 *
 */

#include <stdio.h>
#include "macros.h"

main()
{

        printf("\nx=%f", MIN(123.45, 678.90));
        printf("\nx=%ld", MIN(123451, 67890));
        printf("\nx=%ld", MIN(67890, 123451));

        printf("\nx=%f", MAX(123.45, 678.90));
        printf("\nx=%ld", MAX(123451, 67890));
        printf("\nx=%d", MAX(12345, 6789));

        printf("\nx=%f", ABS(-123.45));
        printf("\nx=%d", ABS(-12345));

        printf("\nx=%d", INT(123.45));
        printf("\nx=%f", FRAC(123.45));
```

```
        printf("\nx=%f", INCH_CM(2));
        printf("\nx=%f", CM_INCH(2));
        printf("\nx=%f", DEG_RAD(15));
        printf("\nx=%f", RAD_DEG(1.56));
        printf("\nx=%f", OZ_GRMS(1.75));
        printf("\nx=%f", GRMS_OZ(28.));
        printf("\nx=%4.2f", HRS_DHRS(12.15));
        printf("\nx=%4.2f", DHRS_HRS(12.50));
        printf("\nx=%f", CRCL_AREA(12.25));
        printf("\nx=%f", RCTNGL_AREA(3.75, 4.05));
        printf("\nx=%f\n", TRNGL_AREA(4.14, 2.23));
}
```

Function Group Two:
Generally Useful Functions

module:	functions:
jul.c	`unsigned int jul()` `main() for demo`

module:	functions:
revjul.c	`char *revjul()` `main() for demo`

module:	functions:
twodates.c	`int two_dates()` `main() for demo`

module:	functions:
zeller.c	`char *zeller()` `main() for demo`

module:	functions:
numbers.c	`void numbers()` `main() for demo`

These functions exploit some of the more powerful data structuring and flow control constructions available in C, particularly the use of arrays of pointers, more standard library functions, and unique-to-C operators.

jul.c

This function performs the more or less "brute force" job of determining the number of days since January 1 of a base year. The number returned is called the Julian date.

The function assumes that the date we are interested in has been entered in the usual format of MM/DD/YY or MM/DD/YYYY, where the slash can be replaced by a hyphen. A pointer to this string is one parameter. The other parameter is the base year.

Sample execution:

```
Enter base year: 1984
Enter date: 12/31/84
366

Enter base year: 1953
Enter date: 5/7/84
11450
```

jul.c

```
/* module title: jul.c
 * function name: unsigned int jul()
 *                main() for demo
 *
 * author: Kim J. Brand
 *
 * revision history:
 *    version/--date--/by reason-------------------------------------------------
 *    1.0   10/01/84 kb Common C Functions initial release
 *
 * compiled with: stdio.h
 * compiled by:
 *
 * linked with:
 * linked by:
 *
 * problems: Julian dates 0 through 3 are reserved for error indicators
 *
 * description: returns the Julian date from the date string based on a base
 *              year given (the year may be 2 or 4 digits, as the function
 *              assumes that 2=digit years < base year are in next century)
 */
```

```
#include <stdio.h>

#define MO 0
#define DAY 1
#define YR 2

#define BAD_DIGIT 0                      /* return error codes        */
#define BAD_MONTH 1                      /* means that the dates      */
#define BAD_DAY 2                        /*  January 1, 2, 3, 4 of the base  */
#define BAD_YEAR 3                       /*  year become invalid dates */

/* #define DEMO */

#ifdef DEMO

main()                          /* small main used for demonstration only  */
{
    char buff[10];              /* to enter strings from console        */
    int base;

    unsigned int jul();

    /* watch for systems that do not flush non-newline terminated strings */
    /* you may need to fflush() after each printf()                       */

    while(1) {
        printf("\nEnter base year: ");
        scanf("%d",&base);
        printf("\nEnter date: ");
        scanf("%s",buff);
        printf("\nJulian date = %u\n",jul(buff,base));
    }
}

#endif

unsigned int jul(date,base)             /* returns unsigned int Julian date */
char *date;                             /*  from string at date in MM-DD-YYYY*/
int base;                               /*  format; Julian base year given by*/
{                                       /*  base; day of year returned if    */
                                        /*  base year same as date year      */

                                        /* make a lookup table for           */
                                        /*  the days in each month           */
                                        /*  indexed by the month in the year */
```

```
static int days[13] = {0, 31, 28, 31, 30, 31, 30, 31, 31, 30, 31, 30, 31};

char c;                          /* an all-purpose character variable */
int n = 0;                       /* starting index in date string     */
int mdy[3];                      /* an array to hold ints for m-d-y    */
unsigned int retjul;             /* becomes the returned value         */

                                 /* start at zero in each 'register'   */

days[2] = 28;                    /* static array is created at         */
                                 /*   compile time and assumed to be   */
                                 /*   permanent; corrects any          */
                                 /*   changes that may have occurred   */
                                 /*   to February                      */


mdy[DAY] = mdy[MO] = mdy[YR] = 0;

while (c = *date++) {             /* get characters from string until  */
                                 /*   end is reached                   */
    if (c == '-' || c == '/') {  /* legal separators are - and /       */
        n++;                     /* index to next element of date      */
        continue;
    }

    if (!isdigit(c))             /* cannot have nonseparators or       */
        return (BAD_DIGIT);      /* nondigits; if so, return now       */

    mdy[n] = 10 * mdy[n] + (c - '0');  /* adds new digit to total      */
                                 /*   for this place                   */
}

if (mdy[MO] < 1 || mdy[MO] > 12)        /* purge bad months           */
    return (BAD_MONTH);

/* if there are only two digits, two-digit years before (19)80        */
/*  are assumed to be in the next century; two-digit years after the  */
/*  base year are assumed to be in this century; the translation      */
/*  becomes (if base == 1980):                                        */
/*      0 - 79 = 2000 - 2079      80 - 99 = 1980 - 1999               */

if (mdy[YR] < 100) {                     /* only two digits?          */
    if (mdy[YR] < base - 1900)           /* prior to base year, digits*/
        mdy[YR] += 2000;                 /*   are assumed to be in the */
    else                                 /*   next century; 01 -> 2001  */
        mdy[YR] += 1900;                 /*   will make 84 -> 1984      */
}
```

```
    if (mdy[YR] < base)                     /* purge bad years            */
        return (BAD_YEAR);

    if (mdy[YR] % 4 == 0 && mdy[YR] % 100 != 0 || mdy[YR] % 400 == 0)
        days[2] = 29;                       /* set February days to 29    */
                                            /*  if leap year              */

    if (mdy[DAY] < 1 || mdy[DAY] > days[mdy[MO]])   /* purge bad days     */
        return (BAD_DAY);

    retjul = mdy[DAY];                      /* set jul equal to days in   */
                                            /*  current month             */

    for (n = 1; n < mdy[MO]; n++) {         /* for every month preceding  */
        retjul += days[n];                  /*  the current one, add days */
    }

    for (n = base; n < mdy[YR]; n++) {      /* now add days from          */
                                            /*  preceding years           */
        if (n % 4 == 0 && n % 100 != 0 || n % 400 == 0)
            retjul += 366;
        else                                /* 365 or 366 based on leaps  */
            retjul += 365;
    }

    return (retjul);

}
```

revjul.c

Complementing the action performed by the jul() function, revjul() turns a Julian date into a date string of the format MM/DD/YY. This function's two parameters are the int Julian date and the int base year.

The function demonstrates the use of initialized static character arrays and several forms of the assignment operators and Boolean logic tests.

Sample execution:

```
Enter Julian date: 11450
Enter base year: 1953
5/7/84


Enter Julian date: 366
Enter base year: 1984
12/31/84
```

revjul.c

```
/*  module title: revjul.c
 *  function name: char *revjul()
 *               main() for demo
 *
 *  author: Kim J. Brand
 *
 *  revision history:
 *    version/--date--/by reason-------------------------------------------
 *      1.0   10/01/84 kb Common C Functions initial release
 *
 *  compiled with: stdio.h
 *  compiled by:
 *
 *  linked with: int twodates()
 *  linked by:
 *
 *  problems:
 *
 *  description: converts a Julian number into a date string
 *
 */
```

```
#include <stdio.h>

#define DEMO

#ifdef DEMO

main()                  /* a simple demonstration main() */
{
    int jul;
    int base;

    char *revjul();

    while (1) {
        printf("\nEnter Julian date: ");
        scanf("%d", &jul);

        printf("Enter base year: ");
        scanf("%d", &base);

        printf("Date = %s\n", revjul(jul,base));
    }

}

#endif

char *revjul(jul,year)              /* returns pointer to string that  */
int jul;                            /*  is calendar date for this      */
int year;                          /*  Julian date in form: mm/dd/yy  */
{
                                    /* number of days in each month    */
                                    /*  indexed by the month in the year */

        static int days[] = {0,31,28,31,30,31,30,31,31,30,31,30,31};

        static char date[11];       /* a place for returned date string */
                                    /*  including the null, must be    */
                                    /*  static or will evaporate       */

        int days_year;             /* the days/year for a given year  */
        int n = 1;                  /* an index into the days/month    */

        setmem(date, sizeof(date), 0);  /* must fill date with nulls so */
                                    /*  strlen knows where date ends   */

        days[2] = 28;               /* fix February if changed         */
```

```
        do {                            /* calculate number of days for   */
                                        /*  base year and all succeeding, */
                                        /*  calculates leap year          */
            if (year % 4 == 0 && year % 100 != 0 || year % 400 == 0)
                days_year = 366;
            else
                days_year = 365;

            year++, jul -= days_year;       /* increment the year and     */

        } while (jul > 0);                  /*  test that does not        */
                                            /*  go over top               */


        year--, jul += days_year;           /* reverse the effect of      */
                                            /*  going too far             */


        if (days_year == 366)               /* if the current year is     */
            days[2] = 29;                   /*  leap, fix February        */

        do                                  /* subtract days from each    */
            jul -= days[n++];               /*  month until jul < 0       */
        while (jul > 0);

                                            /* n holds month number       */
        --n, jul += days[n];                /* jul has day of month       */

        year = (year > 1999 ? year : year - 1900);

        sprintf(date, "%d/%d/%d", n, jul, year);   /* at date build string */

        return (date);                      /* that returns a pointer     */
                                            /*  to the string             */
    }
```

twodates.c

This function is simply a repackaging of an existing function, jul(),
with a little front-end work. To get the days between two dates, all
you have to do is determine each Julian date, based on a common
year (here we have used 1900), and then find the absolute value of
the difference of the two dates.

Sample execution:

```
date 1: 8/8/1985
Enter date 2: 6/3/1953
Days between dates = 11754

Enter date 1: 7/4/1985
Enter date 2: 7/4/1920
Days between dates = 23741

Enter date 1: 7/4/85
Enter date 2: 7/4/20
Days between dates = 23741

Enter date 1: ^C
```

twodates.c

```
/*  module title: twodates.c
 *  function name: int two_dates()
 *                 main() for demo
 *
 *  author: Kim J. Brand
 *
 *  revision history:
 *     version/--date--/by reason-------------------------------------------
 *        1.0   10/01/84 kb Common C Functions initial release
 *
 *  compiled with: stdio.h, macro.h
 *  compiled by:
 *
 *  linked with: unsigned int jul()
 *  linked by:
 *
 *  problems: won't work on dates < 1900 unless base date (1900) is changed
 *
 *  description: calculates the days between two dates by finding the Julian
 *               date of each (using a common base year of 1900) and
 *               returns the absolute value of the dates' difference; if a
 *               bad date is supplied, the function returns a -1
 *
 */

#include <stdio.h>
#include "macros.h"

#define BAD_DATE -1             /* an error code   */

#define DEMO


#ifdef DEMO

main()                                 /* a demonstration main     */
{
    char buff_1[40];           /* a place to enter date strings   */
    char buff_2[40];

    while (1) {
        printf("\nEnter date 1: ");
        scanf("%s", buff_1);
```

137

```
        printf("Enter date 2: ");
        scanf("%s", buff_2);

        printf("Days between dates = %d\n", twodates(buff_1, buff_2));
    }
}

#endif


int twodates(str1,str2)              /* find the days between two dates       */
char *str1;
char *str2;
{
        int jul1;
        int jul2;

        int jul();

        if ((jul1 = jul(str1, 1900)) < 4)        /* 0,1,2,3 are error codes   */
            return (BAD_DATE);                   /*  from Julian date routine */

        if ((jul2 = jul(str2, 1900)) < 4)
            return (BAD_DATE);

        return (ABS(jul1 - jul2));               /* want just the difference  */

}
```

zeller.c

This function provides the useful capability of determining on which day of the week a particular date will fall (or has fallen). With the function, you can construct calendars, create appointment lists by day of the week, etc. The single parameter passed to the zeller() function is a pointer to a string, which gives the date. To be compatible with the date you enter for the MS-DOS DATE prompt, the format of this date string is MM/DD/YY or MM/DD/YYYY. The slash may be replaced by a hyphen. A small main() function is included for demonstration purposes.

Sample execution:

    Enter date: 5/7/53

Sample output:

    Thursday

zeller.c

```
/* module title: zeller.c
 * function name: char *zeller()
 *                main() for demo
 *
 * author: Kim J. Brand
 *
 * revision history:
 *    version/--date--/by reason-----------------------------------------
 *       1.0   10/01/84 kb Common C Functions initial release
 *
 * compiled with: stdio.h, macros.h
 * compiled by:
 *
 * linked with:
 * linked by:
 *
 * problems:
 *
 * description: produces Zeller congruence, given a pointer to the date
 *              string passed, in the format MM/DD/YY or MM/DD/YYYY, and
 *              returns a pointer to a string indicating the day of the week
 *              that the date falls on (the separator may also be a hyphen)
 */
```

```
#include <stdio.h>
#include "macros.h"

#define MO 0
#define DAY 1
#define YR 2

#define BAD_DIGIT 0                     /* error code returned if the date  */
                                        /*  cannot exist                    */
#define DEMO

#ifdef DEMO

main()                      /* this main for demonstration     */
{                           /*  purposes only                  */

        char buff[40];                  /* a place to build input  */

        char *zeller();

        printf("\nEnter date: ");
        scanf("%s", buff);

        printf("%s", zeller(buff));     /* print the day of the week for the */
}                                       /*  date entered                     */

#endif


char *zeller(date)          /* receive pointer to date string; return  */
char *date;                 /*  pointer to day-of-week string          */
{
        char c;                         /* all-purpose character variable   */
        int n = 0;                      /* starting index in input string   */
        int month;                      /* temporary variables              */
        int year;                       /*  with obvious uses               */
        int century;
        int offset;                     /* offset of year in century        */
        int mdy[3];                     /* array holding the three values   */
                                        /*  created from input string:      */
                                        /*  month, day, year                */

        static char *day[] = {          /* pointer to d-o-w string is       */
                "Sunday",               /*  returned from this initialized  */
                "Monday",               /*  array of pointers to chars      */
                "Tuesday",
                "Wednesday",
                "Thursday",
                "Friday",
                "Saturday"
        };
```

```
        mdy[DAY] = mdy[MO] = mdy[YR] = 0;        /* initialize array values   */

        while(c = *date++) {                     /* parse string, through to end   */

            if(c == '-' || c == '/') {  /* legal separators are '-', '/'    */
                n++;                             /* index to next element of date   */
                continue;                        /* (m->d->y) when see one     */
            }

            if(!isdigit(c))                      /* cannot have nonseparators/   */
                return (BAD_DIGIT);              /* nondigits; return error now   */

            mdy[n] = 10 * mdy[n] + (c - '0');    /* adds new digit to total   */
                                                 /* for this place, a very    */
        }                                        /* simplified atoi() that    */
                                                 /* relies on ascii sequence  */

        if(mdy[YR] < 100)
            mdy[YR] += 1900;                     /* accept 2-digit dates      */
                                                 /* for this century          */
        if(mdy[MO] > 2) {
            month = mdy[MO] - 2;                 /* adjust year and month     */
            year = mdy[YR];                      /* based on February         */
        }
        else {
            month = mdy[MO] + 10;
            year = mdy[YR] - 1;
        }

        century = year / 100;                    /* century as 2-digit number */
        offset = year % 100;                     /* years into century        */

/*   these print statements were used for debugging
 *
 *       printf("\ncentury = %d, year = %d, offset = %d", century, year,
 *              offset);
 *       printf("\nmonth = %d, mdy[MO] = %d, mdy[DAY] = %d", month, mdy[MO],
 *              mdy[DAY]);
 */
                                                 /* a magic formula for which */
                                                 /* we must give credit to    */
                                                 /* Zeller                    */

        n = INT((13 * month - 1) / 5) + mdy[DAY] + offset
                + INT(offset / 4) + INT(century / 4) - 2 * century + 77;
        n = n - 7 * INT(n / 7);

        return (day[n]);                         /* returns the pointer       */

}
```

numbers.c

This handy function converts a number into its equivalent written representation, which may be required for a check writer. The function handles numbers up to 999,999,999.99. (If you should need greater size than that, I would like to talk to you about a consulting engagement.)

The function demonstrates some fancy array manipulations, as all the words that make up the final string are located in initialized arrays of pointers to chars. The number itself provides an index into an array, depending on the decade at which the digit is located. The function even decodes teens and numbers that end in even hundreds.

Sample execution:

```
Enter a number: 12345.67
twelve thousand three hundred forty five and 67/100

Enter a number: 98765.43
ninety eight thousand seven hundred sixty five and 43/100

Enter a number: 89010.15
eighty nine thousand ten and 15/100

Enter a number: 17005.00
seventeen thousand five and 00/100

Enter a number: 17005
seventeen thousand five and 00/100
```

numbers.c

```
/*  module title: numbers.c
 *  function name: void numbers()
 *                 main() for demo
 *
 *  author: Kim J. Brand
 *
 *  revision history:
 *     version/--date--/by reason-----------------------------------------
 *        1.0   10/01/84 kb Common C Functions initial release
 *
 *  compiled with: stdio.h, math.h (if you have this header)
 *  compiled by:
 *
 *  linked with: log10() (may be part of a special math library)
 *  linked by:
 *
 *  problems: The string placed in the buffer passed to numbers is not checked
 *            for length, so the buffer must be longer than any potential
 *            string. The current buffer length is 80 characters, and the
 *            current precision for the output is 2 decimal places. These
 *            digits are not spelled out but placed in front of '/100' as
 *            you might use on a check.
 *
 *  description: returns a pointer to a string that spells out the value of the
 *               float the function was passed, as would be used for a
 *               check writer; main() exits when 0 or invalid input is entered
 *               as the number
 */

#include <stdio.h>

#define DEMO

#ifdef DEMO

main()                          /* a simple demonstration main()            */
{
    char buffer[80];            /* space for the number string wanted       */
    double n;                   /* number that is converted                 */
    char num[15];

    void numbers();
    double atof();
    char *fgets();

    for (;;) {
        printf("\nEnter a number: ");          /* enter any number         */
```

```
        fgets(num, sizeof(num)-1, stdin);      /* approved method of        */
        n = atof(num);                         /*  receiving input from user*/

        if (!n)                                /* a zero?                   */
                exit(0);                       /* finished                  */

        setmem(buffer, 80, 0);                 /* initiate buffer with nulls*/

        numbers(n, buffer);                    /* pass to numbers a float   */
                                               /*  and a pointer to buffer  */
                                               /*  to put the result in     */
        puts(buffer);"                         /* print it                  */
    }
}

#endif


void numbers(value, buffer)      /* convert value into string at buffer as  */
double value;                    /*  for a check writer                     */
char *buffer;
{
                        /* these arrays of pointers to character strings are */
                        /*  used to compose the resulting string             */

        static char *units[] = {               /* can initialize only       */
            "",                                /*  static arrays            */
            "one ",
            "two ",
            "three ",
            "four ",
            "five ",
            "six ",
            "seven ",
            "eight ",
            "nine "
        };

        static char *teens[] = {
            "ten ",
            "eleven ",
            "twelve ",
            "thirteen ",
            "fourteen ",
            "fifteen ",
            "sixteen ",
            "seventeen ",
            "eighteen ",
            "nineteen "
        };
```

```
static char *tens[] = {
    "",
    "",
    "twenty ",
    "thirty ",
    "forty ",
    "fifty ",
    "sixty ",
    "seventy ",
    "eighty ",
    "ninety "
};

static char *orders[] = {
    "",
    "thousand ",
    "million "
};

char *ptr;                          /* will be where ascii         */
                                    /*   string is worked on       */
int size;                           /* turns into the number of digits */
int range;

char *malloc();
char *strchr();
double log10();
char *strcat();
char *strncat();

ptr = malloc(20);                   /* make some space             */
if (!ptr) {
    puts("can't allocate space for ptr");
    exit(1);
}

sprintf(ptr, "%-f", value);         /* make an ascii string appear */
                                    /*   in the work space with default */
                                    /*   precision                 */

size = log10(value);                /* returns the number of digits */
                                    /*   before the decimal place  */
                                    /* result truncated to int by assignment */

range = size/3;                     /* 0 if < 1000, 1 < 1,000,000  */
size++;                             /* now up to the real number of digits */
```

145

```
if (value >= 1.0) {            /* as long as number is > 1.0         */
  do {
     if (!(size % 3)) {        /* to check for an even 'order'       */
        strcat(buffer, units[*ptr-'0']);
        if (*ptr++ != '0' )                  /* puts 'hundred' into       */
            strcat(buffer, "hundred ");      /*  buffer if digit was not 0*/
        size--;
     }

     if ((size - 1) % 3) {           /* check for more than one        */
                                     /*  digit in front of natural place */
                                     /*  for comma because             */

        if (*ptr == '1') {           /*  teens are handled differently */
                                     /*  from other number pairs       */

            strcat(buffer, teens[(*++ptr) - '0']);  /* have to pre-inc  */
        }
        else {                       /* regular number pairs handled here */

            strcat(buffer, tens[*ptr++ - '0']);
            if (*ptr != '0' )
                strcat(buffer, units[*ptr - '0']);
        }
        ptr++;                       /* cause had two digits           */
        size -= 2;
     }
     else {
        strcat(buffer, units[*ptr++ - '0']);   /* only a single digit  */
        size--;
     }

     strcat(buffer, orders[range]);

                                          /* if next range is       */
                                          /* all spaces, skip       */
     if ((*ptr | *(ptr + 1) | *(ptr + 2)) == '0' ) {  /* note bitwise OR   */
        range--;
        ptr += 3;
        size -= 3;
     }

  } while (range--);

  strcat(buffer, "and ");
}
                                          /* add the 'nn/100' part   */
strncat(buffer,(strchr(ptr, '.')) + 1, 2);
strcat(buffer, "/100");

}
```

Function Group Three:
User I/O Functions

module: functions:

  window.c   void window()
                                    void scroll()
                                    main() for demo

module: functions:

  menu.c   int menu()
                                    int display()
                                    void h_setup()
                                    void v_setup()
                                    int hit()

module: functions:

  report.c   void report()
                                    main() for demo

modules: functions:

  scan.h   void scan()
                                    void update()
  main.c   void toggle_attribute
                                    int compare_mask()
  scan.c   void reprint()
                                    main() for demo

This group of functions continues the trend toward generality of purpose and complexity. You will recognize more control over the scope of functions and the use of I/O redirection, structures and unions, and initializers.

The following modules are also a part of this group. It is suggested that these modules be included in your own library.

modules:	functions:
adv.c	char *adv()
at_say.c	void at_say()
blank.c	void blank()
bump.c	void bump()
charstr.c	char *char_str() char *center()
getnlin.c	int getnlin() .
get_time.c	void get_time()
incharms.c	int inchar() void outchar()
incharux.c	int initch() int endch() int inchar() int outchar()
place.c	void place()
setcurs.c	void set_cursor()
setmem.c	void setmem()
shift.c	void shr_string() int shl_string()
sindex.c	void sindex()

window.c

This function can add excitement to your dull programs by creating a window within the middle of a screen and allowing you to scroll (up or down) lines of text. Two versions are available, selected by setting the IBM flag to TRUE or FALSE. If set to True, the program will use the hardware-dependent interrupt call (in the IBM BIOS) that scrolls a region of the screen for you. If set to False, the program will use ANSI or non-ANSI command sequences to blank the new line, move the existing lines up or down, and print the new line. (As you can imagine, the latter method is much slower.)

A growing number of utility and application programs use windowing as a method of placing temporary information on the screen. Although this function isn't as sophisticated as such programs, it automatically manages a FIFO list of display lines and will work for both up and down scroll. (This function lacks the ability to preserve the screen's contents that were displayed before the window was drawn.)

Given the window() function, it should be easy to adapt its use to simple on-screen directories, help files, brief lists, etc., which you may want to make a part of your next program. With a little extra effort (and a knowledge of your hardware environment), the function can be modified to take advantage of alternate screens to allow true "pop up" windows that can come and go without destroying the existing data on a screen.

window.c

```
/*  module title: window.c
 *  function name: void scroll(), window()
 *                 main() for demo
 *
 *  author: Kim J. Brand
 *
 *  revision history:
 *     version/--date--/by reason------------------------------------------
 *        1.0   10/01/84 kb Common C Functions initial release
 *
 *  compiled with: stdio.h
 *  compiled by:
 *
 *  linked with: void blank(), place(), setmem()
 *               int getnlin()
 *  linked by:
 *
 *  problems:  If IBM functionality is desired, the row and column addresses
 *             must be 0,0 based instead of 1,1 based, as they are for ANSI
 *             compatibility. If you use another terminal type, you are on your
 *             own and should make adjustments in the place() function. If
 *             IBM is selected, you do not need the blank function.
 *
 *  description: This function scrolls a FIFO window area UP or DOWN,
 *               as defined by the upper row, left column, window width, and
 *               max number of lines.
 *               The function requires direct cursor addressing and takes
 *               advantage of the clear-to-end-of-line feature of the
 *               terminal. Strings are passed as an array of pointers to
 *               window (like *argv[]). After the last line is entered, the
 *               getnlin function starts placing string pointers in the 0
 *               array element again; intervening calls to window have
 *               scrolled the original up or down out of the window by then.
 */

#include <stdio.h>

#ifndef TRUE
#define TRUE 1
#endif

#ifndef FALSE
#define FALSE 0
#endif
```

```
/* #define C86 */                        /* C86 calls the LATTICE function  */
                                         /*  int86() by sysint(); let this  */
#ifdef C86                               /*  macro switch them              */
#define int86(x, y, z) sysint(x, y, z)
#else
#undef max                               /* function wants to use max as a  */
                                         /*  variable name; LATTICE wants to */
#endif                                   /*  use it as a macro              */

#define LFT_COL 30                       /* left edge of window         */
#define TOP_ROW 2                        /* top edge                    */
#define MAX_LINES 16                     /* number of lines in window   */
#define WIDTH 40                         /* width of window             */

#define CLS "\033[2J"                    /* terminal-dependent clear-screen  */
#define CLEOL "\033[0K"                  /*  and clear-to-end-of-line       */

#define UP TRUE                          /* flag tells window to scroll up   */
#define DOWN FALSE                       /* flag tells window to scroll down */

#define IBM TRUE                         /* says can use ROM-BIOS call  */
#define VIDEO_INT 0x10                   /* where to call it at         */
#define ATRIB 0x07                       /* the ROM-BIOS attribute to use */

main()                      /* this main exercises the window function for  */
{                           /*  demonstration purposes                      */

        int n = 0;                               /* begins at 0         */
        int i;                                   /* an all-purpose integer */
                                                 /*  variable           */
        void setmem();
        void place();
        void window();
        int getnlin();
        char *malloc();

        char *line[MAX_LINES];                   /* pointers to 16 lines */

        puts(CLS);                               /* clear screen         */

        for (i = 0; i < MAX_LINES; i++) {        /* initialize pointer values */
            line[i] = malloc(WIDTH + 1);         /*  to point to free space   */
            setmem(line[i], WIDTH + 1, 0);       /* fill line with nulls      */
        }
```

```
        place(TOP_ROW - 1, LFT_COL - 1);           /* set off the box         */
        putchar('+');
        place(TOP_ROW - 1, LFT_COL + 1 + WIDTH);
        putchar('+');
        place(TOP_ROW + MAX_LINES, LFT_COL - 1);
        putchar('+');
        place(TOP_ROW + MAX_LINES, LFT_COL + 1 + WIDTH);
        putchar('+');

        while (1) {
            place(24, 1);                           /* stay out of the way of the*/
                                                    /*  window area demonstration*/
            printf(CLEOL);                          /* blank the input line      */
            printf("Enter another line: ");

            if (getnlin(line[n++], WIDTH))          /* get WIDTH # chars into    */
                break;                              /* line[n], draw all         */

            window(TOP_ROW, LFT_COL, WIDTH, MAX_LINES, UP, line);

            n %= MAX_LINES;                         /* creates a circular  */
                                                    /*  buffer            */

        }
}
void window(row, col, width, max, dir, line)        /* define window by left/top */
int row, col, width, max, dir;                      /*  edge, width, max lines   */
char *line[];                                       /*  and whether fill is      */
{                                                   /*  top-down or bottom-up    */

        int n;                                      /* all-purpose integer       */
        int temp;                                   /* likewise a-p integer      */
        static int start = 0;                       /* first time through        */
                                                    /*  start = 0; thereafter    */
                                                    /*  retains the last value   */
                                                    /*  stored there, reminds user*/
                                                    /*  where next line goes      */

#if IBM
        void scroll();
        void place();


        scroll(dir, row, col, max, width);          /* row is fixed based on dir */
        place((dir ? row + max - 1 : row), col);
        puts(line[start]);

#else

        void place();
        void blank();
```

```
        row = (dir ? row + max - 1 : row);       /* row is fixed based on dir */

        for (temp = start, n = 0; n < max; n++) {
            blank(row, col, width);              /* clear the line             */
            place((dir ? row-- : row++), col);   /* position the cursor        */
            puts(line[temp--]);                  /* print the line             */
            temp += max, temp %= max;            /* create a circular buffer   */
        }

#endif

        start++;                                 /* next line is advanced */
        start %= max;                            /* but not too far       */
}

#if IBM

void scroll(dir, row, col, max, width)       /* for a PC video display    */
int dir;                                     /* scroll this way:          */
unsigned int row, col;
int max, width;
{
        struct {                                 /* structure needed for      */
            int ax, bx, cx, dx, si, di, ds, es;  /* system-interrupt call     */
        } sreg;

        sreg.ax = (dir ? 0x0600 : 0x0700) + 1;   /* direction gives int       */
                                                 /* command plus lines to     */
                                                 /* move                      */
        sreg.bx = ATRIB;                         /* attribute on new line     */
                                                 /* set the row/col           */
        sreg.cx = (row - 1 << 8) + col - 1;      /* -1 because pf int call    */
                                                 /* positioning vs. ANSI,     */
                                                 /* the ! subtracts an extra  */
                                                 /* line when moving down     */
        sreg.dx = (row - 1 + max - !dir << 8) + col + width - 1;

        int86(VIDEO_INT, &sreg, &sreg);

}

#endif
```

menu.c

This function can be quite useful both for constructing a menu of choices on the user console and for accepting a choice. Selections may be displayed horizontally or vertically. A parameter passed to the function selects the style to use and allows both styles (horizontal and vertical) to be used in the same program. The user selects a menu item (1) by pressing a letter (or number) corresponding to the first character of the choice, or (2) by moving a highlighted window (or other video attribute) over the items by pressing the space bar and picking an item by pressing RETURN.

You will notice that the terminal control strings used to turn on the desired highlighting are #defined at the top of the source module. Unfortunately, terminals from different manufacturers, and sometimes even different models from the same manufacturer, make use of incompatible control sequences. The result is heavily screen-oriented programs that become quite complicated as they attempt to be user-configurable for a variety of terminals. This program accommodates both ANSI and non-ANSI-type terminals, specifically the TeleVideo 910. The ANSI terminal-emulation capability of the IBM PC was used for testing.

To work, the ANSI.SYS driver must be made resident by placing the line device = ANSI.SYS in the CONFIG.SYS file and by having the file ANSI.SYS located in the root directory of your boot disk.

You will also notice the use of a function, inchar(), that retrieves a single character from the user console without echo. This capability is typically forgotten in most standard libraries and is supplied in the module. The feature, however, is quite environment dependent. You should examine carefully the code presented and determine for yourself if it will work unmodified for you.

This function heavily uses pointers to functions and makes use of the memory allocation functions calloc() and free(), to demonstrate how space can be created "on the fly" to locate arrays.

Sample execution:

With hv set to VERT:

    A Function 1
    B. Function 2
    C Function 3

With hv set to HORIZ:

A Function 1   **B. Function 2**   C Function 3

Every press of the space bar will move the underscore (or other highlighting attribute) to the next menu item in a circular manner. Pressing the RETURN key selects the item where the underscore has stopped, as does pressing the key corresponding to the first letter of the menu item—in this case an A, B or C.

menu.c

```
/*   module title: menu.c
 *   function names: int menu(), display(), hit()
 *                   void h_setup(), v_setup(), toggle()
 *
 *   author: Kim J. Brand
 *
 *   revision history:
 *      version/--date--/by reason-------------------------------------------------
 *        1.0   10/01/84 kb Common C Functions initial release
 *
 *   compiled with:
 *   compiled by:
 *
 *   linked with: int inchar()
 *                void place()
 *   linked by:
 *
 *   problems: Because the attributes are hard coded, the existing display modes
 *             (especially foreground or background colors) are overwritten
 *             with the attributes chosen. A more useful (and complex) approach
 *             would be to determine the existing attribute and 'OR' or
 *             'AND' the highlighting attribute with the attribute, turning it
 *             on and off, respectively.
 *
 *   description: Function constructs general-purpose menu-selection screens,
 *                the spread can be horizontal or vertical. An item is selected
 *                by pressing the return key after the highlighting window
 *                has been moved over its name with the space bar (or other key)
 *                or the first character of the window's name is pressed.
 *
 */
```

```
#include <stdio.h>

#ifndef TRUE
#define TRUE 1
#endif

#ifndef FALSE
#define FASE 0
#endif

#define ANSI TRUE                       /* uses ANSI escape sequences if TRUE*/

#define HORZ 0                          /* flags that select a horizontal    */
#define VERT 1                          /*  or vertical menu display,         */
#define ON 1                            /*  specify whether to turn           */
#define OFF 0                           /*  attributes on or off,             */
#define SPACING 3                       /*  spacing between columns in        */
                                        /*  horz_disp                         */


#if ANSI

#define LEFT_ATTRIB "\033[4m"           /* terminal control strings for  */
#define RIGHT_ATTRIB "\033[0m"          /*  for start/stop underscore in */
                                        /*  ANSI                         */

#else

#define LEFT_ATTRIB "\033G4"            /* terminal control strings         */
#define RIGHT_ATTRIB "\033G0"           /*  for start/stop reverse video,   */
                                        /*  used to highlight selection;    */
                                        /*  these were used for a Televideo */
                                        /*  910 and are terminal dependent  */

#endif


#define HDISP_ROW 20                    /* starting display row for horizon- */
#define HDISP_WIDE 80                   /*  tal display, width of screen     */
#define VDISP_COL 30                    /* starting col for vertical display */
#define VDISP_ROW 5                     /* starting row for vertical display */

#define ESCAPE '\033'                   /* used to get back from display     */
                                        /*  menus without making a selection */
#define DEMO

struct choice {                         /* structure holds a pointer to      */
        void (*function)();             /*  a function, name of structure    */
        char *name;                     /*  is displayed in the menu         */
};
```

```
struct edges {                          /* to store cursor positions    */
        char row;                       /*  calculated on the fly       */
        char left_col;                  /*  in horz_disp, vert_disp     */
        char right_col;
};


#ifdef DEMO

main()                  /* small demonstration main to get started    */
{
        int ret;

        void func1();                   /* sample functions selected by
        void func2();                   /*  menu and executed by reference to*/
        void func3();                   /*  their position in the array of   */
                                        /*  structures containing their      */
                                        /*  address (pointer)                */

        static struct choice selection[] = {    /* creating an array of      */
            {func1, "A Function 1"},             /*  structs in memory,      */
            {func2, "B Function 2"},    /* initialized with pointers to      */
            {func3, "C Function 3"},    /*  functions and their names,       */
            {0},                        /*  this null marks the end          */
        };                              /*  (static so it can be initialized)*/

        int menu();


        printf("\nNow executing function %x:\n", ret = menu(selection, VERT));

        (*selection[ret].function)();           /* invokes chosen function  */
}

#endif


int menu(ptr, hv)                       /* create a menu and wait for       */
struct choice ptr[];                    /*  input, return integer           */
int hv;                                 /*  corresponding to item selected  */
{
        int n;
        int ret;
        char **str;                             /* pointers to the name str */
                                                /*  pointers                */
        int display();
        char *calloc();

        for (n = 0; ptr[n].function; n++)       /* calculates number of */
            ;                                   /*  structures          */
```

```
                                          /* produce a pointer        */
        str = (char **)calloc(n, sizeof(char *));
                                       /*  to where the pointers go */
                                       /*  while making space for   */
                                       /*  the pointers             */
        if (!str) {
            puts("error allocating space for str");
            exit(1);
        }


        for (n = 0; ptr[n].function; n++)    /* for every function       */
            str[n] = ptr[n].name;            /*  required, initialize a  */
                                             /*  pointer to its name in  */
                                             /*  this special []!        */


        ret = display(str, n, hv);     /* does the display           */
                                       /*  whether horizontal or vertical  */
                                       /*  and returns the one wanted     */

        free(str);

        return (ret);

}

int display(str,n,hv)                  /* displays strings horiz or vert   */
                                       /*  and the user chooses one,       */
                                       /*  returns 0-n being the chosen one */
char *str[];                           /* strings to print            */
int n;                                 /* number of strings           */
int hv;                                /* flag to tell whether horz or vert */
{
        int i, pick;
        char c;
        struct edges *loc;             /* hold the cursor positions of     */
                                       /*  the edges of each string in this */
                                       /*  array of structures             */

        int (*hv_setup[2])();          /* makes space for pointers to two  */
                                       /*  functions that set up the       */
                                       /*  edges for accent around where the*/
                                       /*  function names are printed      */

        char *calloc();
        void place();
        void toggle();
        int hit();
        void h_setup();
        void v_setup();

        hv_setup[0] = h_setup;         /* plant the address of the         */
                                       /*  horizontal setup function,      */
        hv_setup[1] = v_setup;         /* address of vertical function     */
```

```
                                    /* make space for the cursor      */
                                    /*  location structure            */

    loc = (struct edges *)calloc(n, sizeof(struct edges));

    if (!loc) {
        puts("error allocating memory for loc");
        exit(1);
    }

    (*hv_setup[hv])(loc, n, str);        /* set up cursor positions    */
                                         /*  based on horz/vert        */

                                    /* now all edges are in structure  */
                                    /*  print the strings              */
    for (i = 0; i < n; i++) {
        place(loc[i].row, loc[i].left_col + 1);
        puts(str[i]);
    }
    fflush(stdout);
                                    /* turn on the attributes around   */
    i = 0;                          /*  loc[0]                         */

    toggle(&loc[i], str[i], LEFT_ATTRIB, RIGHT_ATTRIB, ON);

                                    /* for each non-hit character,      */
                                    /*  remove the window from where we */
                                    /*  are and put it where we're going */

    while ((c = inchar()) != ESCAPE && c != '\r') {
        if ((pick = hit(str, c, n)) >= 0)
            break;
        toggle(&loc[i], str[i], LEFT_ATTRIB, RIGHT_ATTRIB, OFF);
        i++, i %= n;
        toggle(&loc[i], str[i], LEFT_ATTRIB, RIGHT_ATTRIB, ON);
    }

    free(loc);

    return (c == ESCAPE ? -1 : (c == '\r' ? i : pick));

}

void h_setup(loc, n, str)
struct edges loc[];
int n;
char *str[];
{
```

```
        int length;
        int line;
        int i;
        int size;
        char c;
        char col;


        for (i = 0, line = HDISP_ROW; i < n; i++) {  /* for number of    */
                                                     /*  strings         */

            length = 1;                              /* current line length   */
            col = 1;                                 /* current column position */

            while ((length + (size = 1 + strlen(str[i]))) < HDISP_WIDE && i < n) {
                loc[i]. row = line;
                loc[i]. left_col = col;
                loc[i]. right_col = col += size;
                col += SPACING;
                length += col;
                i++;
            }
            i--;                                     /* get back to previous item */
            line++;                                  /* move down to next line    */
        }
}

void v_setup(loc, n, str)
struct edges loc[];
int n;
char *str[];
{
        int line, i;
        char c;

        for (i=0, line = VDISP_ROW; i < n; i++) {        /* for the number    */
            loc[i]. row = line;                          /* of strings        */
            loc[i]. left_col = VDISP_COL;
            loc[i]. right_col = VDISP_COL + strlen(str[i]) + 1;
            line++;
        }


}

void func1()             /* need dummy functions so can take     */
{                        /*  their address                       */
        printf("function one\n");
}
```

```
void func2()
{
        printf("function two\n");
}


void func3()
{
        printf("function three\n");
}


int hit(str, c, n)
char *str[];
char c;
int n;
{
        int i = -1;                             /* failure is assumed         */

        c = toupper(c);                         /* always compare with caps  */

        while (n--) {
            if (c == toupper(*str[n])) {         /* if find c as the first    */
                i = n;                           /*   character of the name   */
                break;                           /*   set i to the one that hit*/
            }                                    /*   break out               */
        }

        return (i);
}

void toggle(ptr, str, lft, rt, flag)            /* function wraps a text string with */
                                                /*  some video attribute, typically  */
                                                /*  reverse video or underlining     */
struct edges *ptr;                              /* where to put them                 */
int flag;                                       /* putting on or taking off flag     */
char *lft;                                      /* the left and right attributes     */
char *rt;
char *str;
{

#if ANSI
        void place();
        int printf();
```

```
        place(ptr -> row, 1 + ptr -> left_col);
        printf("%s%s%s%s",(flag ? lft : rt), str, (!flag ? rt : lft), rt);

                                        /* final right attribute makes   */
                                        /*  leave with underscore        */
                                        /*  (or other attribute) off     */

        fflush(stdout);
#else
        void place();
        int puts();

        char *attribute[2];             /* by setting up this small   */
        char position[2];               /*  array, can select         */
                                        /*  attributes by index;      */
        position[0] = ptr -> left_col;  /* because only two, can let  */
        position[1] = ptr -> right_col; /*  a logical operator        */
        attribute[0] = lft;             /*  select what is first,     */
        attribute[1] = rt;              /*  with non-ANSI terminals   */
                                        /*  it matters                */

        place(ptr -> row, position[flag]);
        flag ? puts(attribute[flag]) : putchar(' ');
        place(ptr -> row, position[!flag]);
        flag ? puts(attribute[!flag]) : putchar(' ');

        fflush(stdout);
#endif

}
```

report.c

The prospect of developing an attractive report-formatting function has often left me settling for second best, or none at all. Therefore, here is a simple-to-use, general-purpose report-printing function that also demonstrates some reasonably complex structure manipulations.

The single report() function actually gets called to do the following separate tasks:

1. Sets up the shape of the report by deciding how wide to make the columns (based on the width of the first column header string), and prints the header complete with column titles on the I/O device selected (either the console or the printer)

2. Prints rows of numbers out of an array of doubles (one per column) and sends prompts for a keystroke to continue if stdout is used (or a page eject if PRN is used) at the end of a screen or page

3. Sums the columns after printing a double row of dashes under each column when instructed

Without having to call three separate functions, you can obtain this versatility by passing to report() a single pointer to structure, containing the following: a flag value to signal the service requested, a union of a structure used to pass setup information, and the address of the array of doubles to be printed.

As with the menu() and amort() functions, an operating-system-dependent function, inchar(), is used to suspend output to the console until a keystroke is entered. Make sure that you confirm that this function will work in your environment. Notice also the use of the fflush() function to get the I/O buffers to dump their data to the screen. This function depends on the screen and the internal program logic being coordinated. If the Press any key to continue message appears in the middle of a column of numbers or if the program stops before the totals have been printed, something is wrong. Both of these symptoms can result from inadequate buffer flushing. (Sounds like a plumbing maintenance manual, doesn't it?)

Sample execution:

string 000	string 1	string 002	string 3
234. 56	876. 54	753. 10	468. 12
234. 56	876. 54	753. 10	468. 12
234. 56	876. 54	753. 10	468. 12
234. 56	876. 54	753. 10	468. 12
234. 56	876. 54	753. 10	468. 12
234. 56	876. 54	753. 10	468. 12
234. 56	876. 54	753. 10	468. 12
234. 56	876. 54	753. 10	468. 12
234. 56	876. 54	753. 10	468. 12
234. 56	876. 54	753. 10	468. 12
234. 56	876. 54	753. 10	468. 12
234. 56	876. 54	753. 10	468. 12
234. 56	876. 54	753. 10	468. 12
234. 56	876. 54	753. 10	468. 12
234. 56	876. 54	753. 10	468. 12
234. 56	876. 54	753. 10	468. 12
234. 56	876. 54	753. 10	468. 12
234. 56	876. 54	753. 10	468. 12
234. 56	876. 54	753. 10	468. 12
234. 56	876. 54	753. 10	468. 12
234. 56	876. 54	753. 10	468. 12

Press any key to continue...

string 000	string 1	string 002	string 3
234.56	876.54	753.10	468.12
234.56	876.54	753.10	468.12
234.56	876.54	753.10	468.12
234.56	876.54	753.10	468.12
234.56	876.54	753.10	468.12
234.56	876.54	753.10	468.12
234.56	876.54	753.10	468.12
234.56	876.54	753.10	468.12
234.56	876.54	753.10	468.12
234.56	876.54	753.10	468.12
234.56	876.54	753.10	468.12
234.56	876.54	753.10	468.12
234.56	876.54	753.10	468.12
234.56	876.54	753.10	468.12
234.56	876.54	753.10	468.12
234.56	876.54	753.10	468.12
234.56	876.54	753.10	468.12
234.56	876.54	753.10	468.12
234.56	876.54	753.10	468.12
234.56	876.54	753.10	468.12
234.56	876.54	753.10	468.12

Press any key to continue...

string 000	string 1	string 002	string 3
234.56	876.54	753.10	468.12
234.56	876.54	753.10	468.12
234.56	876.54	753.10	468.12
234.56	876.54	753.10	468.12
234.56	876.54	753.10	468.12
234.56	876.54	753.10	468.12
234.56	876.54	753.10	468.12
234.56	876.54	753.10	468.12
234.56	876.54	753.10	468.12
234.56	876.54	753.10	468.12
234.56	876.54	753.10	468.12
234.56	876.54	753.10	468.12
234.56	876.54	753.10	468.12
234.56	876.54	753.10	468.12
234.56	876.54	753.10	468.12
234.56	876.54	753.10	468.12
234.56	876.54	753.10	468.12
234.56	876.54	753.10	468.12
234.56	876.54	753.10	468.12
234.56	876.54	753.10	468.12
234.56	876.54	753.10	468.12
234.56	876.54	753.10	468.12

Press any key to continue...

string 000	string 1	string 002	string 3
234.56	876.54	753.10	468.12
234.56	876.54	753.10	468.12
234.56	876.54	753.10	468.12
234.56	876.54	753.10	468.12
234.56	876.54	753.10	468.12
==========	==========	==========	==========
16419.20	61357.80	52717.00	32768.40

report.c

```
/*  module title: report.c
 *  function name: void report()
 *                 main() for demo
 *
 *  author: Kim J. Brand
 *
 *  revision history:
 *     version/--date--/by reason-------------------------------------------
 *        1.0   10/01/84 kb Common C Functions initial release
 *
 *  compiled with: stdio.h
 *  compiled by:
 *
 *  linked with: char *char_str(), int inchar()
 *  linked by:
 *
 *  problems: If the console or printer I/O streams return an error when
 *            the function is opened for writing, the function aborts with
 *            an exit(). A total that exceeds the width of its column
 *            will mess up the output; choose a header string long enough.
 *
 *  description:
 *     This function decodes the first member (flag) of the structure to
 *     which the function's single parameter points and determines whether
 *     the invocation is a setup, print, or total command. Based on this
 *     information, the structure contents are used to set up page width,
 *     height, offset (from the left margin), number of rows per page, I/O
 *     device, and number of columns of printing. If the flag indicates
 *     that values should be printed, a pointer to an array of pointers to
 *     to doubles accesses values to be printed in each column. If the flag
 *     indicates the end, totals are printed at the bottom of each column.
 *
 *     Hard coded into the function are the facts that formatted conversions
 *     of numbers should be made with "%10.2f". (The System V C compiler
 *     printf() function accepts run-time-determined conversion parameters
 *     and can be added if your compiler supports this feature.)
 *
 *     All columns are assumed to be the same width, and their associated
 *     header strings are gauged by the header for the first column. This
 *     header must be at least 10 characters wide; if other headers are
 *     narrower, they are right-justified within the space allowed.
 */
```

```
#include <stdio. h>              /* required because I/O selection is */
                                 /*  made based on a parameter passed */

struct info_block {
    int flag;                    /* this flag determines how the      */
                                 /*  following pointer is interpreted */
    union {                      /* the union supports passing        */
        struct init_block {      /*  either pointer to the init_block */
            int io_device;       /*  structure or to the array of     */
            int columns;         /*  doubles                          */
            int offset;
            int page_width;
            int rows_per_page;
            char **header_string;
        } *set_up;
        double *value;
    } on;
};                               /* no identifier means no definition */
                                 /*  and keeps the structure          */
                                 /*  from being global                */


#define init info->on. set_up    /* these simplify lengthy            */
#define device copy->io_device   /*  data access constructions        */

#define SETUP 1                  /* setup, total, and vals command    */
#define VALS 0                   /*  assigned to flag that tells      */
#define TOTAL 2                  /*  function information there       */

#define TERM_PAGE '\0'           /* terminal page eject               */
#define LIST_PAGE 0xc            /* printer page eject                */
#define TERM_LINES 24
#define LIST_LINES 56


#define MAX_HEAD 132             /* maximum space allocated for       */
                                 /*  header string                    */


#define NUM_LENGTH 10            /* field width of numbers            */
#define COL_SPACE 3              /* space between columns             */

#define DEMO

#ifdef DEMO

main()                           /* a demonstration main()            */
{
        int n;                   /* all-purpose integer variable      */
        struct info_block *info; /* pointer to structure of type      */
                                 /*  info_block                       */
        char *string[4];         /* array of four (uninitialized)     */
                                 /*  pointers to character strings    */
        double number[4];        /* likewise for four doubles         */
```

```
void report();
char *malloc();


string[0] = "string 000";          /* create column titles          */
string[1] = "string 1";
string[2] = "string 002";
string[3] = "string 3";

number[0] = 234.56;                 /* and data                      */
number[1] = 876.54;
number[2] = 753.10;
number[3] = 468.12;

                                    /* make room for structures in memory*/
                                    /* convince compiler that what   */
                                    /*  malloc returns is a pointer to   */
                                    /*  these structure types         */

info = (struct info_block *)malloc(sizeof(struct info_block));
init = (struct init_block *)malloc(sizeof(struct init_block));

if (!info || !init) {
    puts("error allocating space for info or init");
    exit(1);
}

info->flag = SETUP;                 /* for setup mode                */

init->io_device = 0;                /* 0=console, otherwise lst      */
init->columns = 4;                  /* 4 columns                     */
init->offset = 5;                   /* page offset of 5 columns      */
init->page_width = 80;              /* console width                 */
init->rows_per_page = TERM_LINES;   /* screen or page height         */
init->header_string = string;       /* address of first member       */
                                    /*  of array of pointers to      */
                                    /*  header strings               */

report(info);          /* pass address of structure to              */
                       /*  report function, this time for setup     */

info->flag = VALS;     /* send the real values                      */

info->on.value = number;            /* point value pointer at array  */
                                    /*  of doubles, which are usually*/
                                    /*  changed during course of     */
                                    /*  program                      */
for (n = 0; n < 70; n++)
    report(info);                   /* print numbers      */

info->flag = TOTAL;
```

```
        report(info);                    /* print the totals   */

        free(init);
        free(info);
}

#endif


void report(info)              /* passed pointer to structure that contains */
struct info_block *info;       /*  setup/value/total command information    */
{
        int n;                          /* all-purpose integer variable     */
        int head_length;                /* length of header                 */
        FILE *fp;

                                        /* the following are static so they */
                                        /*  are remembered                  */
        static int max_length;          /* column width calculated from     */
                                        /*  first column header string,     */
        static int length_dif;          /* difference between maximum        */
                                        /*  column width and number field,  */
        static struct init_block *copy; /* copy of init_block pointer        */
        static double *total;           /* place where totals are kept,     */
                                        /*  accessed like an array          */
                                        /*  after size is determined,       */
        static char *head, *toe;        /* likewise for the head/toe strings */
        static char eject;              /* terminals & printers have unique  */
                                        /*  pagination commands              */
        static int rows = 3;            /* start on line 3: header, two      */
                                        /*  blank lines                      */

        FILE *fopen();
        char *calloc();
        char *malloc();
        char *strcat();
        char *char_str();

        if (info->flag == SETUP) {      /* check to see whether numbers     */
                                        /*  or setup or total command       */

            fp = fopen((init->io_device) ? "PRN" : "CON", "w");
            if (!fp) {
                puts("error opening output stream");
                exit(1);
            }

            copy = init;                /* copy pointer to            */
                                        /*  init struct for later use; */
                                        /*  assume that data is still in */
                                        /*  memory after setup call   */
```

```
                                    /* make space for array of     */
                                    /* doubles: total[], cast result so */
                                    /* compiler will not complain   */

total = (double *)calloc(copy->columns, sizeof(double));

                                        /* initialize start values  */
for (n = 0; n < copy->columns; n++)
    total[n] = 0.0;
                                    /* set up eject code for pages  */

eject = (device) ? LIST_PAGE : TERM_PAGE;

                                /* send 1 to start */

putc(eject, fp);
                                    /* create 1 heading string from */
                                    /* the several received         */

head = malloc(MAX_HEAD);    /* assume head is not > MAX_HEAD */
toe = malloc(MAX_HEAD);     /* space for the underlines     */
if (!head || !toe) {
    puts ("can't allocate space for head/toe");
    exit(1);
}
*head='\0', *toe='\0';      /* init first position of each so */
                            /* strcat knows where to start   */

max_length = strlen(copy->header_string[0]);        /* biggest */
length_dif = max_length - NUM_LENGTH;

                                    /* insert number of spaces equal */
                                    /* to offset from left           */

strcat(head, char_str(copy->offset, ' '));
strcat(toe, char_str(copy->offset, ' '));

                                    /* make up a header string from the */
                                    /* pieces, and the toe string       */

for (n=0; n < copy->columns; n++) {
    head_length = strlen(copy->header_string[n]);

    strcat(head, char_str(max_length - head_length, ' '));
    strcat(head, copy->header_string[n]);
    strcat(head, char_str(COL_SPACE, ' '));

    strcat(toe, char_str(length_dif, ' '));
    strcat(toe, char_str(NUM_LENGTH, '='));
    strcat(toe, char_str(COL_SPACE, ' '));

}
```

```
                                    /* print header and two newlines,  */
                                    /* now on row 2, (0,1,2)           */

      fprintf(fp, "%s\n\n", head);

}
else if (info->flag == TOTAL) {          /* the total command           */

      fprintf(fp, "%s\n", toe);          /* mark each column with '=' */
                                         /* and add margin, next line*/

      fprintf(fp, "%s", char_str(copy->offset, ' '));

      for (n=0; n < copy->columns; n++) { /* the totals               */

          fprintf(fp, "%s", char_str(length_dif,' '));
          fprintf(fp, "%10.2f%s", total[n], char_str(COL_SPACE, ' '));
      }

      putc('\n', fp);                    /* add newline at end          */
      fflush(fp);

      free(total);                       /* don't be piggish because    */
      free(head);                        /* you're done now             */
      free(toe);
      if (fp != stdout)                  /* going to a real file?       */
          fclose(fp);                    /* close it                    */

}
else {                    /* print another line of numbers            */

      if (rows++ == copy->rows_per_page) {     /* eject when get        */
                                               /* too many lines;       */
          if (!device)     {                   /* if console, pause*/
              fprintf(fp, "Press any key to continue");
              fflush(fp);
              inchar();                        /* stop until a          */
                                               /* key pressed,          */
                                               /* then erase it         */
              fprintf(fp, "\r                  \n");
          }
          putc(eject, fp);
          rows = 3;                            /* and print header      */
                                               /* plus 2 newlines       */
          fprintf(fp, "%s\n\n", head);
      }
                                  /* print the numbers here     */

      fprintf(fp, "%s", char_str(copy->offset, ' '));
      for (n = 0; n < copy->columns; n++) {
```

```
        fprintf(fp, "%s", char_str(length_dif, ' '));
        fprintf(fp, "%10.2f%s", info->on.value[n], char_str(COL_SPACE, ' '));
        total[n] += info->on.value[n];
    }

    putc('\n', fp);                           /* add newline at end        */

}
}
```

scan.c

This function is the most complicated one in the book and also the most valuable. Of all the functions for sale or available in the public domain, this function is one of the most generally useful and complex. The function prints a prompt and requests an input in a manner similar to the dBASE II command:

@ row,col say "prompt" get variable picture "mask"

scan() is more flexible, however, and complements the standard library scanf() function by adding the following features:

1. Six masks that control input

2. A field width display using either characters and / or video attributes selectable per field

3. Numeric entry with fixed decimal point (as in DataStar)

4. Multiple entry fields retrievable with a single call, with independent prompts and locations on the screen

5. Right-justified entry for both numeric and alphabetical variables

6. The contents of a variable prior to the call can optionally be displayed in the field

7. A help string displayed at a different location on the screen

8. My famous "disappearing prompt" that optionally makes the prompt for a particular field go away as soon as entry is started so that the space the prompt took can be used as part of the entry window

The function works like the scanf() function, but scan() uses an array of structures with six values to describe as many input field windows as are required. Only a pointer to the first structure is passed to the function:

```
struct _scan {
        char row, col;          /* where to put it                     */
        char *mask;             /* mask-formatting characters          */
        char *prompt;           /* message in field that may get moved */
        char *help;             /* the help message                    */
        char *field;            /* place where data ends up            */
        char width;             /* the width of the entry field        */
};
```

where:

row is the row address, from 0 to 23 or 24

col is the column address, absolute from 0 to 79

mask is a pointer to a mask/conversion string

%[f, d, s] - like scanf() and printf(), followed
by a sequence of mask characters

single position effect:

9 - accept only a numeric character, a period (.), or a
minus sign (-)
A - accept only an alpha character
X - accept any alphanumeric character
! - make any alpha character uppercase
. - locate the decimal point

entire entry effect:

[- use video attributes for highlighting
| c - use c as the field window character (spaces are
the default)
* - ring bell if bad character tried or if entry full
> - right-justify entry
@ - display current value in variable
^ - wait for carriage return when field full; otherwise,
go to the next field automatically
< - replace the entry prompt with more field space

field is the address of a variable to fill with the data just as in
scanf(); the variable gets cast to the right type when we know
what it is

prompt is a pointer to the string we want to print as the prompt

help is the message that you want to appear when the field is
reached; its location is independent of the entry field

width is the field input width

Note: As a practical matter, the f format indicates a double;
the d format, a long integer; and the s format, a pointer to a
character string.

One of the unfortunate realities of the current crop of microcomputer systems (at least those that aspire to be compatible
with the IBM PC) is the "distance" between the console and the

program that wants to write to it. In other words, the distance is the overhead associated with character I/O. This function was originally written for use on a CP/M system. The heavy requests for cursor positioning and character moving were not even noticeable. But when I ported the function to an IBM PC, a character deletion took so long that I thought the processor had stopped. The cause stems from the ability of DOS to redirect console I/O, which complicates the console driver, and the impact of ANSI.SYS, which I was using to achieve environment independence. These features, added to the buffered I/O by the compiler, made `putchar()` and `getchar()` unacceptable for such an application.

In this function, I have thrown caution to the wind and implemented "direct to the interrupt level" capabilities that give performance the priority it must have in heavy user I/O functions. The result is nonportable but should be easily adaptable, given an architecture similar to the IBM PC's. If you are running under CP/M or another environment in which system interrupt calls are unavailable, you can modify the offending functions (as noted in the header) to perform similar actions in your domain. The most unique feature of the IBM is its use of memory-mapped video. Most of the system dependencies in `scan()` relate to printing a string at a particular place on the console and then adding or deleting a video attribute (such as reverse video, half intensity, etc.).

In my use of this function for implementing multiple data entry screens to support a moderate-sized data base application, the user reaction has been good. The increase in the number of fields capable of being displayed on a single screen by using my "disappearing prompt" improves data entry performance and creates a much cleaner display. The help string has also proved to be quite useful. In the actual implementation, I added special facilities for moving between blocks of fields; for moving to the next unfilled field; for moving to the next page, the previous page, or a user-selected page; and for constant display of the system time/ date.

scan.h

```
/*
 * Include file for scan function
 */

#define END 100
#define ON 1
#define OFF 0

#define UP_ARROW 0x748
#define DOWN_ARROW 0x750
#define LEFT_ARROW 0x74b
#define RIGHT_ARROW 0x74d
#define BACKUP 0x8
#define DELETE 0x18
#define CLEAR 0x747
#define VIDEO_INT 0x10
#define PGUP 0x749

#define ON_ATTR 0x0f
#define OFF_ATTR 0x07

#define BACKSPACE '\b'
#define BELL '\007'
#define RETURN '\r'

#define HELP_ROW 22
#define HELP_COL 1

#define OFFSET(n) (data[n].cursor_col-data[n].min_column)

struct _scan {
        char row, col;          /* where to put it                 */
        char *mask;             /* mask-formatting characters      */
        char *prompt;           /* message in field that is moved   */
        char *help;
        char *field;            /* place where data ends up         */
        char width;             /* the width of the entry field     */
                                /* following are set by install     */
};
```

```
struct _data {
        char *mask_character;
        char *entry_chars;
        char attribute;
        char field_character;
        char dot_location;
        char cursor_col;
        char min_column;
        char max_column;
        char data_type;
        char ring_flag;
        char right_flag;
        char show_flag;
        char dot_flag;
        char dot_yet;
        char full_flag;
        char data_yet;
        char replace;
};

struct _sreg {
    int ax, bx, cx, dx, si, di, ds, es;
};
```

main.c

```
/*  module title: main.c
 *  function names: main() (demo for scan() function)
 *
 *  author: Kim J. Brand
 *
 *  revision history:
 *     version/--date--/by reason-----------------------------------------
 *        1.0   10/01/84 kb Common C Functions initial release
 *
 *  compiled with: stdio.h, ctype.h, scan.h
 *  compiled by:
 *
 *  linked with: int scan()
 *  linked by:
 *
 *  problems:
 *
 *  description: a demo front end for the scan function, places nine
 *               fields on the screen with representative combination of
 *               most of the features of scan()
 *
 */

#include <stdio.h>
#include <ctype.h>
#include "scan.h"

#define CLS "\033[2J"                          /* ANSI terminal clear code */

struct _rec1 {
        char idno[10];  /* identification number */
        char actv[ 2];  /* active status */
        char name[31];  /* name */
        char adr1[31];  /* address */
        char ctyf[17];  /* city */
        char stat[ 3];  /* state */
        char date[ 9];  /* date */
        long tagn;      /* tag */
        float amnt;     /* amount */
} rec1;

struct _scan scrn1[] = {
        { 1, 1, "%s*|\372[XXXXXXXXX", "I.D.# ", "Enter the Customer I.D number",
                rec1.idno, 9},
        { 1,70, "%s*^|\372[!", "Status: ", "Enter A:Active, C:Closed", rec1.actv, 1},
        { 2,25, "%s*@<|\372[XXXXXXXXXXXXXXXXXXXXXXXXXXXXXX", "Name",
                "Enter the customer's name", rec1.name, 30},
```

```
            { 4, 1,  "%s*<|\372[XXXXXXXXXXXXXXXXXXXXXXXXXXXXXX", "address", "Enter the
                     customer's address", rec1.adr1, 30},
            { 5, 1,  "%s*<|\372[XXXXXXXXXXXXXXX", "city", "Enter the customer's city,
                     town, or location", rec1.ctyf, 16},
            { 5,19,  "%s*<|\372[!!", "st", "Enter the customer's state of residence",
                     rec1.stat, 2},
            { 5,23,  "%s*<|\372[99/99/99", "date", "Enter the date of purchase",
                     rec1.date, 8},
            { 6, 1,  "%d*^>|\372[99999999", "tag: ", "Enter the customer's tag number",
                     (char *)&rec1.tagn, 8},
            { 6,15,  "%f@^*|\372[99999.99", "amount: ", "Enter the amount of the sale",
                     (char *)&rec1.amnt, 8},
            {END}
};

main()
{
        int scan();
        char *strcpy();

        puts(CLS);

        strcpy(rec1.name,"Brand, Kim J.");        /* to demonstrate that       */
                                                  /*  default value display    */
                                                  /*  feature really works     */

        scan(scrn1);

        puts("\n\nFinal values:");

        printf("rec1.idno = %s\n",rec1.idno);
        printf("rec1.actv = %s\n",rec1.actv);
        printf("rec1.name = %s\n",rec1.name);
        printf("rec1.adr1 = %s\n",rec1.adr1);
        printf("rec1.ctyf = %s\n",rec1.ctyf);
        printf("rec1.stat = %s\n",rec1.stat);
        printf("rec1.date = %s\n",rec1.date);
        printf("rec1.tagn = %ld\n",rec1.tagn);
        printf("rec1.amnt = %8.2f\n",rec1.amnt);

}
```

scan.c

```
/*  module title: scan.c
 *  function names: void reprint(), scan(), toggle_attributes(), update()
 *                  int compare_mask()
 *
 *  author: Kim J. Brand
 *
 *  revision history:
 *    version/--date--/by reason------------------------------------------
 *      1.0   10/01/84 kb Common C Functions initial release
 *
 *  compiled with: stdio.h, ctype.h, scan.h
 *  compiled by:
 *
 *  linked with: int inchar(), sindex()
 *               char *adv(), *shl_string(), *shr_string()
 *               void place()
 *  linked by:
 *
 *  problems:  The high frequency of console I/O demanded by this function
 *             requires the use of the nonportable I/O functions:
 *
 *                  place()          set_cursor()
 *                  bump()           inchar()
 *                  outchar()        at_say()
 *
 *             The program will probably work with little or no modification
 *             as long as the target machine includes I/O interrupt services
 *             similar to those of the IBM PC. (The program was developed on
 *             an NEC APC-III.)
 *
 *             Right-justified fields should not be given masks that contain
 *             special characters ('/' or '-') or masks with a combination
 *             of types ('999XXAA') because the input string is shifted left
 *             with each new entry and the input verification always fails.
 *
 *  description: implements a form of the dBASE II command:
 *
 *                  @ x,y say 'string' get 'variable' picture 'mask'
 *
 *             can produce a data entry screen with prompts,
 *             highlighted windows with various entry options,
 *             and context-sensitive help
 */
```

```
#include <stdio.h>
#include <ctype.h>
#include "scan.h"

#ifndef TRUE
#define TRUE 1
#endif

#ifndef FALSE
#define FALSE 0
#endif

#define C86                              /* to permit use of nonstandard     */
                                         /*  library functions that          */
                                         /*  give access to the interrupt    */
                                         /*  system and BIOS calls           */

#define OTHER                            /* option uses standard library     */
                                         /*  memory allocation               */

#ifdef OTHER

#define getmem(x) malloc(x)              /* getmem is complemented by rlsmem */
                                         /*  for LATTICE C. C86 and most other*/
                                         /* C compilers use malloc and free  */


#endif

#ifdef C86                               /* memory allocation method called  */

#define int86(x,y,z) sysint(x,y,z)       /* other changes for going to C86   */
#define intdos(x,y) sysint21(x,y)        /* note: C86 requires -us flag for  */
#define atol(x) atoi(x)                  /*  compiling this and other modules */
                                         /*  that use it                     */

#endif


struct _data *data;                      /* pointer to array of temporary    */
                                         /*  structures used to hold data    */


int scan(ptr)                            /* the scan function                */
struct _scan ptr[];
{
        static char space[80];           /* place to store input characters  */
        char *work_space;                /* auto pointer to input characters */

        int c;                           /* local character holder, must be  */
        int temp;                        /*  int so large scan codes can be  */
                                         /*  returned                        */
```

```
        int n;                          /* counters                 */
        int i;
        int j;

        int fields;                     /* stores number of fields  */
        char *mask_ptr;                 /* local copy of a pointer to the */
                                        /*  mask string, speeds things up */

        char *getmem();
        char *strcpy();
        int sindex();
        void at_say();
        void bump();
        void place();
        void reprint();
        void set_cursor();
        void toggle_attributes();
        void update();
        void wrt_chrs();
        int shl_string();
        void shr_string();
        void outchar();
        int inchar();
        int compare_mask();

#ifdef OTHER
        int free();
#else
        int rlsmem();
#endif

        for (i = 0; ptr[i].row != END; i++)
            ;                           /* find out how many elements are */
                                        /* in the scan structure          */
        fields = i;

        data = (struct _data *)getmem(i * sizeof(struct _data));
        if (!data) {
            puts("getmem data failed");
            exit(1);
        }
        setmem(data, i * sizeof(struct _data), 0);

                                        /* for each field, make a place for */
                                        /*  and initialize its data structure*/
        for (i = 0; i < fields; i++) {
            data[i].mask_chars = getmem(ptr[i].width+1);
            data[i].entry_chars = getmem(ptr[i].width+1);
            if (!data[i].mask_chars || !data[i].entry_chars) {
                puts("getmem mask_chars or entry_chars failed");
                exit(1);
            }
```

```
        setmem(data[i].mask_chars, ptr[i].width + 1, 0);
        setmem(data[i].entry_chars, ptr[i].width + 1, 0);
        data[i].attribute = FALSE;
        data[i].field_character = '\040';
        data[i].ring_flag = FALSE;
        data[i].right_flag = FALSE;
        data[i].show_flag = FALSE;
        data[i].dot_flag = FALSE;
        data[i].dot_yet = FALSE;
        data[i].full_flag = FALSE;
        data[i].data_yet = FALSE;
        data[i].replace = FALSE;
        data[i].max_column = 0;
    }

    set_cursor(0);                          /* determine all the      */
    for (n = 0; n < fields; n++) {          /*  options selected and set */
        mask_ptr = ptr[n].mask;             /*  flags for each field  */
                                            /* increment through the mask*/
        i = 0;
        while (c = *mask_ptr++) {
            switch (c) {
                case '.':
                    data[n].dot_location = i;    /* fixed characters   */
                    data[n].dot_flag = TRUE;     /*  in the mask have  */
                default:                         /*  bit 7 set as a tag*/
                    c |= 0x80;
                case '9':                        /* all special        */
                case 'A':                        /*  characters are put*/
                case 'X':                        /*  in local mask     */
                case '!':
                    data[n].mask_chars[i++] = c;
                    ++data[n].max_column;
                    break;

                case '%':                        /* marks the type     */
                    data[n].data_type = *mask_ptr++;
                    break;

                case '[':                        /* indicates window   */
                    data[n].attribute = TRUE;
                    break;

                case '|':                        /* marks the field    */
                    data[n].field_character = *mask_ptr++;
                    break;

                case '*':                        /* want bells         */
                    data[n].ring_flag = TRUE;
                    break;
```

```
            case '>' :                          /* right-justified  */
                data[n].right_flag = TRUE;
                break;

            case '~' :                          /* <cr> required    */
                data[n].full_flag = TRUE;
                break;

            case '@' :                          /* use default value */
                data[n].show_flag = TRUE;
                break;

            case '<' :                          /* replace prompt   */
                data[n].replace = TRUE;         /*  with field      */
                break;
        }
    }

    data[n].cursor_col = data[n].min_column =
        ptr[n].col + strlen(ptr[n].prompt);

    if (data[n].replace)
        data[n].max_column += ptr[n].col;
    else
        data[n].max_column += data[n].min_column;

                                        /* cause existing value in    */
                                        /*  variable to show if desired */
    setmem(work_space = (char *)space, 80, 0);
                                        /* init work_space to point at space */

    j = 0;
    while (c = data[n].mask_chars[j])
        data[n].entry_chars[j++] = (c & 0x80) ? c & 0x7f : '\040';

    if (data[n].show_flag) {    /* show any pre-existing value */
        switch(data[n].data_type) {
            case 'd' :          /* a long */
                if (*(long int *)ptr[n].field != 0)
                    data[n].data_yet = TRUE;
                sprintf(work_space, "%ld", *(long int *)ptr[n].field);
                if (data[n].right_flag)
                    j = strlen(data[n].entry_chars) - strlen(work_space);
                else
                    j = 0;
                goto move_it;
```

```
                     case 'f':              /* a float */
                         if (*(float *)ptr[n].field != 0)
                             data[n].data_yet = TRUE;
                         sprintf(work_space, "%8.2f", *(float *)ptr[n].field);
                         j = data[n].dot_location - sindex(work_space,'.');
                         goto move_it;

                     case 's':              /* a string */
                         if (strlen(ptr[n].field) && strcmp(ptr[n].field, data[n].entry_chars))
                             data[n].data_yet = TRUE;
                         strcpy(work_space, ptr[n].field);
                         if (data[n].right_flag)
                             j = strlen(data[n].entry_chars) - strlen(work_space);
                         else
                             j = 0;

move_it:             while (c = *work_space++)
                         data[n].entry_chars[j++] = c;
                     break;
            }
        }
    reprint(&ptr[n], n, OFF_ATTR);         /* print field contents   */
                                           /* print opening prompt    */

    if (!data[n].replace || !data[n].data_yet)
        at_say(ptr[n].row, ptr[n].col, ptr[n].prompt, OFF_ATTR);

                              /* adjust opening cursor position   */
                              /* based on field contents          */
    if (data[n].dot_flag)
        data[n].cursor_col = data[n].min_column + data[n].dot_location;
    else if (data[n].right_flag)
        data[n].cursor_col = data[n].max_column;
    else if (data[n].replace && data[n].data_yet) {
        for (i = ptr[n].width - 1; data[n].entry_chars[i] == '\040'; i--)
            ;
        data[n].cursor_col = ptr[n].col + i + 1;
        data[n].min_column = ptr[n].col;
    }
    else
        data[n].cursor_col = data[n].min_column;
}

set_cursor(1);                             /* turn cursor on         */
n = 0;                                     /* set up the first       */

toggle_attributes(ON, &ptr[n], n);
place(ptr[n].row, data[n].cursor_col);
```

```
        while ((c = inchar()) != EOF) {
            switch (c) {
                case UP_ARROW:                              /* when move out of  */
up:                 toggle_attributes(OFF, &ptr[n], n);     /* field, turn off   */
                    update(&ptr[n], n);                     /* attributes        */
                    if (--n < 0)                            /* and turn on next  */
                        n = 0;                              /* one's             */
                    toggle_attributes(ON, &ptr[n], n);
                    place(ptr[n].row, data[n].cursor_col);
                    break;

                case RETURN:
ret:
                case DOWN_ARROW:
down:               toggle_attributes(OFF, &ptr[n], n);
                    update(&ptr[n], n);
                    if (++n == fields)
                        goto goback;

                    toggle_attributes(ON, &ptr[n], n);
                    place(ptr[n].row, data[n].cursor_col);
                    break;

                case LEFT_ARROW:
left:               if (!data[n].dot_flag && !data[n].right_flag) {
                        if (--data[n].cursor_col < data[n].min_column) {
                            data[n].cursor_col = data[n].min_column;
                            goto up;
                        }
                        if (*(data[n].mask_chars + OFFSET(n)) & 0x80)
                            --data[n].cursor_col;
                        place(ptr[n].row, data[n].cursor_col);
                    }
                    break;

                case RIGHT_ARROW:
right:              if (!data[n].dot_flag && !data[n].right_flag) {
                        if (++data[n].cursor_col >= data[n].max_column) {
                            data[n].cursor_col = data[n].min_column;
                            goto down;
                        }
                                /* note that fixed characters in field    */
                                /*  use bit 7 as a flag                   */
                        if (*(data[n].mask_chars + OFFSET(n)) & 0x80)
                            ++data[n].cursor_col;
                        place(ptr[n].row, data[n].cursor_col);
                    }
                    break;
```

```
                case CLEAR:
clear:              i = 0;
                while (c=data[n].mask_chars[i])
                    data[n].entry_chars[i++] = (c & 0x80) ? c & 0x7f : '\040';
                data[n].data_yet = FALSE;
                if (data[n].dot_flag) {
                    data[n].cursor_col = data[n].min_column + data[n].dot_location;
                    data[n].dot_yet = FALSE;
                    strcpy(&data[n].entry_chars[data[n].dot_location - 1], "0.00");
                }
                else if (!data[n].right_flag) {
                    if (data[n].replace)
                        data[n].cursor_col = data[n].min_column + strlen(ptr[n].prompt);
                    else
                        data[n].cursor_col = data[n].min_column;
                }
                reprint(&ptr[n], n, ON_ATTR);
                if (data[n].replace)
                    at_say(ptr[n].row, ptr[n].col, ptr[n].prompt, ON_ATTR);
                break;

            case BACKUP:
            case DELETE:
                if (!data[n].data_yet)
                    break;

                if (data[n].dot_flag) {      /* handle a f.p. number   */
                    if (!data[n].dot_yet) {
                        shr_string(data[n].entry_chars, '.');
                        reprint(&ptr[n], n, ON_ATTR);
                    }
                    else {
                        if (data[n].dot_location < --data[n].cursor_col -
                                data[n].min_column) {
                            place(ptr[n].row, data[n].cursor_col);
                            outchar(data[n].field_character);
                            place(ptr[n].row, data[n].cursor_col);
                            *(data[n].entry_chars + OFFSET(n)) = '\040';
                        }
                        else {
                            data[n].dot_yet = FALSE;
                            place(ptr[n].row, (data[n].cursor_col =
                                    data[n].dot_location + data[n].min_column));
                        }
                    }
                }
                else {                       /* handle other types here */
                    if (data[n].right_flag) {
                        shr_string(data[n].entry_chars, '\0');
                        reprint(&ptr[n], n, ON_ATTR);
                    }
```

```
                    else {
                        if (--data[n].cursor_col < data[n].min_column)
                            goto clear;
                        else {
                            if (*(data[n].mask_chars + OFFSET(n)) & 0x80)
                                --data[n].cursor_col;
                            place(ptr[n].row, data[n].cursor_col);
                            outchar(data[n].field_character);
                            place(ptr[n].row, data[n].cursor_col);
                            *(data[n].entry_chars + OFFSET(n)) = '\040';
                        }
                    }
                }
                break;

        case '.':                           /* decimal point is special  */
            if (data[n].dot_flag) {     /* if in dot_flag            */
                if (!data[n].dot_yet) {          /* true field, else */
                    data[n].dot_yet = TRUE;      /* drop into        */
                    goto right;                  /* default case     */
                }
            }
            else if (data[n].data_type == 'd') {  /* cannot have    */
                if (data[n].ring_flag)            /* decimal point  */
                    outchar(BELL);                /* in int field   */
                break;
            }


        default:               /* all other inputs here */
            if (!data[n].data_yet && data[n].replace) {
                data[n].cursor_col = data[n].min_column = ptr[n].col;
                reprint(&ptr[n], n, ON_ATTR);
                data[n].data_yet = TRUE;
            }
            else
                data[n].data_yet = TRUE;

                                /* all this work is used to        */
                                /* place cursor correctly on screen */
                                /* and edit incoming entries        */
            if (data[n].dot_flag) {
                if (isdigit(c) || c == '-') {
                    if (!data[n].dot_yet) {
                        shl_string(data[n].entry_chars, c, '.');
                        reprint(&ptr[n], n, ON_ATTR);
                    }
```

```
            else {
                if (data[n].dot_location < OFFSET(n)) {
                    if (data[n].cursor_col < data[n].max_column) {
                        outchar(c);
                        *(data[n].entry_chars + OFFSET(n)) = c;
                        data[n].cursor_col++;
                    }
                    if (data[n].cursor_col == data[n].max_column) {
                        if (data[n].ring_flag)
                            outchar(BELL);
                        if (!data[n].full_flag)
                            goto ret;
                    }
                }
                else {
                    bump();
                    outchar(c);
                    *(data[n].entry_chars + (++data[n].cursor_col -
                                data[n].min_column)) = c;
                    data[n].cursor_col++;
                }
            }
        }
    else
        if (data[n].ring_flag)
            outchar(BELL);
}
else {
    if (data[n].right_flag) {
        shl_string(data[n].entry_chars, c, '\0' );
        if (compare_mask(data[n].mask_chars, data[n].entry_chars))
            reprint(&ptr[n], n, ON_ATTR);
        else {
            shr_string(data[n].entry_chars, '\0' );
            if (data[n].ring_flag)
                outchar(BELL);
        }
        if (*data[n].entry_chars != '\040' ) {
            if (data[n].ring_flag)
                outchar(BELL);
            if (data[n].full_flag)
                goto ret;
        }
    }
```

```
                    else {
                        if (data[n].cursor_col < data[n].max_column) {
                            temp = *(data[n].entry_chars + OFFSET(n));
                            *(data[n].entry_chars + OFFSET(n)) = c;
                            if (compare_mask(data[n].mask_chars, data[n].entry_chars)) {
                                place(ptr[n].row, data[n].cursor_col);
                                outchar(*(data[n].entry_chars + OFFSET(n)));
                                data[n].cursor_col++;
                            }
                            else {
                                *(data[n].entry_chars + OFFSET(n)) = temp;
                                if (data[n].ring_flag)
                                    outchar(BELL);
                            }
                            if (*(data[n].mask_chars + OFFSET(n)) & 0x80) {
                                data[n].cursor_col++;
                                bump();
                            }
                        }
                        if (data[n].cursor_col >= data[n].max_column) {
                            if (data[n].ring_flag)
                                outchar(BELL);
                            if (!data[n].full_flag)
                                goto ret;
                        }
                    }
                }
                break;
            }
        }
                                /* give back memory used     */
goback:
        for (n = 0; n < fields; n++) {

#ifdef C86
            free((char *)data[n].mask_chars);
            free((char *)data[n].entry_chars);
#else
            if (rlsmem((char *)data[n].mask_chars, ptr[n].width + 1)) {
                printf("error deallocating mask_chars, fields=%d, n=%d",fields,n);
                exit(1);
            }
            if (rlsmem((char *)data[n].entry_chars, ptr[n].width + 1)) {
                printf("error deallocating entry_chars, fields=%d, n=%d",fields,n);
                exit(1);
            }
#endif
        }
```

```
#ifdef C86
        free((char *)data);
#else
        if (rlsmem((char *)data, fields * sizeof(struct _data))) {
            puts("error deallocating data");
            exit(1);
        }
#endif

        return (c);                /* so know what happened */
}

void reprint(ptr,n,attr)          /* fills a field window with value that */
struct _scan *ptr;                /* has been entered into its buffer     */
int attr;
int n;
{
    int j;
    static char extra[80];

    char *strcpy();
    void at_say();
    void place();

    if (!data[n].data_yet) {                    /* if no data yet */
        strcpy(extra, data[n].entry_chars);

        for (j = 0; extra[j]; j++) {
            if (extra[j] == '\040')
                extra[j] = data[n].field_character;
        }

        if (data[n].replace)
            at_say(ptr->row, ptr->col, extra, attr);
        else
            at_say(ptr->row, data[n].min_column, extra, attr);
    }
    else {
        if (data[n].replace)
            at_say(ptr->row, ptr->col, data[n].entry_chars, attr);
        else
            at_say(ptr->row, data[n].min_column, data[n].entry_chars, attr);
    }

    place(ptr->row, data[n].cursor_col);

}
```

```
int compare_mask(test,given)           /* makes sure entry is valid */
char *test;
char *given;
{
        char c;
        char obj;

        while (c = *test++) {
            obj = *given++;

            if (obj == '\040')
                continue;

            switch (c) {
                case '9' :
                    if (!isdigit(obj) && obj != '-' && obj != '.')
                        return (FALSE);
                    break;

                case 'A' :
                    if (!isalpha(obj))
                        return (FALSE);
                    break;

                case 'X' :
                    if (!isprint(obj))
                        return (FALSE);
                    break;

                case '!' :
                    *(given - 1) = toupper(obj);
                    break;


            }
        }
        return (TRUE);
}

void toggle_attributes(flag,ptr,n)      /* adds or deletes a highlighting   */
int flag;                               /*  window around an entry field    */
struct _scan *ptr;                      /* puts a help line at a fixed       */
int n;                                  /*  location                         */
{
        struct _sreg sreg;
        int temp;
        unsigned int row, col;

        void place();
        void at_say();
```

```
if (data[n].attribute) {                      /* change attribute of    */
                                              /* what is already there  */

    row = ptr->row;
    col = ptr->col;

    for (temp = data[n].max_column - col; temp; temp--, col++) {

        place(row, col);

        sreg.ax = 0x0800;              /* read character/attribute at cursor*/
        sreg.bx = 0;

        int86(VIDEO_INT, &sreg, &sreg);
                                              /* if moving into field     */
                                              /*  and character is space, */
                                              /*  replace character with  */
                                              /*  field_character to      */
                                              /*  define th field width   */

        if (flag && ((sreg.ax & 0x00ff) == '\040') && col >= data[n].min_column)
            sreg.ax = data[n].field_character | 0x0900;
        else if (!flag && ((sreg.ax & 0x00ff) == data[n].field_character)
            && data[n].data_yet)
            sreg.ax = '\040' | 0x0900;
        else
            sreg.ax = (sreg.ax & 0x00ff) | 0x0900;   /* write same       */

        sreg.bx = (flag ? ON_ATTR : OFF_ATTR);
        sreg.cx = 1;

        int86(VIDEO_INT, &sreg, &sreg);

    }
}

if (flag)                                      /* write new help line    */
    at_say(HELP_ROW, HELP_COL, ptr->help, ON_ATTR);
else {
    place(HELP_ROW, HELP_COL);
    wrt_chrs('\040', strlen(ptr->help));       /* clear help line        */
}
}
```

```
void update(ptr, n)          /* loads destination variable with      */
struct _scan *ptr;           /*  current contents of appropriate field */
int n;
{
        long atol();
        double atof();
        char *strcpy();
        char *adv();

        switch (data[n].data_type) {
            case 'd' :
                *(long int *)ptr -> field = atol(adv(data[n].entry_chars));
                break;
            case 'f' :
                *(float *)ptr -> field = atof(adv(data[n].entry_chars));
                break;
            case 's' :
                strcpy(ptr -> field, data[n].entry_chars);
        }
}
```

Library Functions

The following functions are used with many other functions in this book. The functions here are suggested for possible inclusion in a hypothetical library, which would be used in the same way as the "standard library" delivered with every C compiler. The linking command would include the name of the library, for example, ccflib, usually just before the name of any other libraries you may want the linker to search as it resolves the external variables and function names referenced in the other parts of your program.

One of the decisions you will face as you construct your own library has to do with the "granularity" you want to achieve. This term pertains to the way the functions have been divided (placed in separately compiled modules) and, therefore, to the minimum amount of code that the linker will include from the library in order to satisfy a single reference. Some compiler publishers go to great lengths to subdivide their library functions into as many modules as possible so that programs which make use of only small parts of the standard library won't be burdened by the size of the portion not used.

You determine your own library granularity by making choices about which functions and how many modules to include. It makes sense to g roup into a single module the functions that work together to provide a single capability. It also makes sense, but can be less convenient, to separate all other functions into their own modules. In this way, the librarian (the program that assembles a library from its component functions) will be able to make entries into its directory for the minimum portion that should be included by the linker when the program is finally assembled.

The suggested library includes the following modules. They are listed opposite the function(s) they include, along with a brief description of purpose:

adv. c	char *adv()	Advances a pointer argument past the leading white space and returns the new pointer
at_say. c	void at_say()	Positions the cursor and writes a string on the user console with a given attribute (IBM PC)

`blank.c`	`void blank()`	Locates the cursor and prints spaces for the number of places given
`bump.c`	`void bump()`	Moves the cursor one position to the right
`charstr.c`	`char *char_str()`	Returns a pointer to a static area, containing a given number of characters as specified
	`char *center()`	Centers a string in a space of specified width by prepending spaces
`getnlin.c`	`int getnlin()`	Retrieves a given number of characters from `stdin`, stopping on receipt of a \n or EOF
`get_time.c`	`void get_time()`	Obtains the time and date from MS-DOS through an interrupt function call
`incharms.c`	`int inchar()`	Retrieves a single character from the user console without echo or waiting for a \n (IBM PC)
	`void outchar()`	Writes a single character to the user console without waiting for a \n (IBM PC)

`incharux.c`	`int initch()`
	`int endch()`
	`int inchar()`
	`int outchar()`
		Same as the previous two functions but designed for UNIX, where single-character I/O is more awkward

`place.c`	`void place()`	Positions the cursor on the user console (IBM PC and others)
`set_curs.c`	`void set_cursor()`	Enables/disables the cursor (IBM PC)

setmem.c	void setmem()	Fills a string (memory) with a given character for a count specified
	void shr_string()	Shifts a string to the right, starting at its leftmost character and stopping at a given character, padding with blanks
	int shl_string()	Shifts a string left into existing spaces, stopping at a given character on right and inserting a given character; returns TRUE if successful, or else FALSE
sindex.c	int sindex()	Returns an integer indicating the offset into a string where a given character is found

adv.c

```
/*  module title: adv.c
 *  function name: char *adv()
 *
 *  author: Kim J. Brand
 *
 *  revision history:
 *     version/--date--/by reason-------------------------------------------
 *        1.0   10/01/84 kb Common C Functions initial release
 *
 *  compiled with:
 *  compiled by:
 *
 *  linked with: int scan()
 *  linked by:
 *
 *  problems:
 *
 *  description: moves a pointer to a string up to the first non-white-space
 *               character therein
 */



char *adv(string)        /* pointer to a string is incremented to first   */
char *string;            /* non-white-space character; note: because the  */
{                        /* parameter is a copy, the actual pointer is not */
                         /* changed                                        */

        while (isspace(*string))
                string++;

        return (string);
}
```

atsay.c

```
/*    module title: at_say.c
 * function names: void at_say()
 *
 * author: Kim J. Brand
 *
 * revision history:
 *    version/--date--/by  reason-----------------------------------------
 *       1.0   10/01/84 kb  Common C Functions initial release
 *
 * compiled with: stdio.h
 * compiled by:
 *
 * linked with: int scan()
 *              void place(), set_cursor()
 * linked by:
 *
 * problems: totally IBM PC-campatible machines (or nearly so like the NEC
 *           APC III) are required due to the use of interrupt functions
 *           required to make this function fast
 *
 * description: the primary means of printing on the user console used
 *              in the scan() function
 */

#include <stdio.h>

struct _sreg {int ax,bx,cx,dx,si,di,ds,es;  };   /* define structure used with */
                                                 /* IBM PC interrupt function */
                                                 /* calls                     */


#define C86                                      /* the interrupt function     */
                                                 /* call is compiler dependent*/
                                                 /* commment this line out if  */
                                                 /* you are using the LATTICE  */
                                                 /* compiler, or else refer    */
                                                 /* to your compiler's docu-   */
                                                 /* mentation                  */


#ifdef C86
#define int86(x,y,z) sysint(x,y,z)
#endif

#define VIDEO_INT 0x10            /* 0x19 for NEC APC-III        */
```

```
void at_say(row,col,ptr,attr)          /* locate the cursor and say        */
unsigned int row,col,attr;             /*  something with a given attribute */
char *ptr;                             /* attributes are defined in the PC  */
{                                      /*  BASIC and Technical Reference doc*/

        struct _sreg sreg;

        int c;

        void place();
        void set_cursor();

    if (*ptr) {                        /* only if there is something there  */
        set_cursor(0);                 /* turn cursor off                   */

        place(row, col++);
        sreg.bx = attr;                /* page number is in the high order  */
                                       /*  8 bits; this might be changed to */
                                       /*  be a passed parameter            */
        sreg.cx = 1;                   /* first character gets written with */
        sreg.ax = 0x0900 | *ptr++;     /*  attribute; the rest are easier   */
        int86(VIDEO_INT, &sreg, &sreg);

        place(row, col);               /* moves cursor one place to right   */

        while (c = *ptr++) {
            sreg.ax = 0x0e00 | c;
            int86(VIDEO_INT, &sreg, &sreg);
        }

        set_cursor(1);                 /* turn cursor back on               */
    }
}
```

blank.c

```
/*  module title: blank.c
 *  function names: void blank()
 *                  void place()
 *
 *  author: Kim J. Brand
 *
 *  revision history:
 *      version/--date--/by reason---------------------------------------
 *          1.0   10/01/84 kb Common C Functions initial release
 *
 *  compiled with:
 *  compiled by:
 *
 *  linked with:
 *  linked by:
 *
 *  problems:
 *
 *  description: place() is a general purpose cursor-positioning function
 *               that can be used with ANSI teminals (including the IBM PC
 *               when the ANSI.SYS file has been declared in CONFIG.SYS,) and
 *               non-ANSI terminals, such as the TELEVIDEO, WYSE-50, and
 *               others. blank() uses same to position the cursor and write
 *               spaces from there for a specified width.
 */

#include <stdio.h>
#include "macros.h"              /* location of the definition of ROW and    */
                                 /*  COL                                     */
#define VIDEO_INT 0x10           /* if use ROM-BIOS calls, need to know      */
                                 /*  where to call it                        */

/* #define C86 */                /* C86 uses a different name for int86,     */
                                 /*  which is the name LATTICE uses.         */
#ifdef C86                       /* provide following macro if C86 is used   */
#define int86(x,y,z) sysint(x,y,z)
#endif


#define IBM                      /* If this line here, ROM-BIOS cursor       */
                                 /*  positioning will be used.               */

#define ANSI                     /* If this line removed, the non-ANSI       */
                                 /*  cursor-positioning scheme will be used. */

#define LEAD_IN "\033="          /* for the non-ANSI terminal we want to     */
                                 /*  support here, lead-in string is an      */
                                 /*  escape (0x1b) followed by an equals sign */
```

```
void blank(row, col, width)        /* start at row, col and for width places   */
int row;
int col;
int width;
{
        void place();

        place(row, col);
        while (width--)
            putchar(' ');
}


void place(row, col)               /* position cursor at row and column given  */
unsigned int row;
unsigned int col;
{

#ifdef IBM

        struct { int ax, bx, cx, dx, si, di, ds, es; } sreg;

        sreg.ax = 0x0200;                          /* for positioning the      */
                                                   /*  cursor                  */

                                                   /* remember to subtract one */
                                                   /*  because ROM-BIOS is 0,0 */
        sreg.dx = (row - 1 << 8) | col - 1;        /* set up row and column    */
        sreg.bx = 0;                               /* page number              */

        int86(VIDEO_INT, &sreg, &sreg);

#else
        int printf();

#ifdef ANSI                                        /* ANSI sequence needs      */
        printf("\033[%d;%dH", row, col);           /*  row and column values in */
                                                   /*  ascii. Remember ANSI    */
                                                   /*  coordinates start at 1, 1. */

#else
        printf(LEAD_IN);                           /* cannot use puts because  */
                                                   /*  adds a newline at end,  */

        putchar(ROW(row));                         /* These macros just adjust */
        putchar(COL(col));                         /*  the row/col base value  */
                                                   /*  to meet terminal's      */
                                                   /*  requirements.           */
#endif
#endif
}
```

bump.c

```
/*    module title: bump.c
 *  function names: void bump()
 *
 *  author: Kim J. Brand
 *
 *  revision history:
 *     version/--date--/by  reason-------------------------------------------
 *       1.0   10/01/84 kb  Common C Functions initial release
 *
 *  compiled with: stdio.h
 *  compiled by:
 *
 *  linked with:
 *  linked by:
 *
 *  problems:
 *
 *  description: if ANSI defined, use the ANSI function for cursor forward;
 *               else use the IBM PC (and comaptibles) ROM-BIOS read cursor/
 *               position cursor functions
 *
 */

#include <stdio.h>

struct _sreg {int ax, bx, cx, dx, si, di, ds, es; };    /* interrupt function call  */
                                                        /*  structure used by LATTICE*/
                                                        /*  and C86               */

#define ANSI                      /* remove for ROM-BIOS functions            */

#define C86                               /* the interrupt function     */
                                          /*  call is compiler dependent*/
                                          /* commment this line out if  */
                                          /* you are using the LATTICE  */
                                          /*  compiler, or else refer   */
                                          /* to your compiler's docu-   */
                                          /* mentation                  */
#ifdef C86
#define int86(x, y, z) sysint(x, y, z)
#endif

#define VIDEO_INT 0x10                    /* 0x19 for NEC APC-III       */

void bump()                               /* move cursor forward one place */
{
#ifdef ANSI

    printf("\033[1C");                    /* easy if ANSI               */
```

```
#else

        struct _sreg sreg;

        sreg.ax = 0x0300;              /* read cursor position command   */
        sreg.bx = 0;                   /* page number                    */

        int86(VIDEO_INT, &sreg,&sreg);

        sreg.dx++;                     /* bump column number in dl by one */
        sreg.ax = 0x0200;              /* set cursor position command    */

        int86(VIDEO_INT, &sreg, &sreg);

#endif
}
```

charstr.c

```
/*   module title: charstr.c
 *   function name: char *char_str()
 *                  char *center();
 *
 *   author: Kim J. Brand
 *
 *   revision history:
 *      version/--date--/by reason------------------------------------------
 *        1.0   10/01/84 kb Common C Functions initial release
 *
 *   compiled with: stdio.h
 *   compiled by:
 *
 *   linked with: void amort()
 *   linked by:
 *
 *   problems: For charstr(), lengths up to only 80 characters are supported
 *             because an internal static array is declared at compile time.
 *             For center(), the maximum field width is 132 characters.
 *
 *   description: charstr() returns a pointer to a string filled with a
 *                given number of a specified character. center() returns a
 *                pointer to a string in which the string argument has been
 *                centered in a specified field width.
 */

#include <stdio.h>

/* #define DEMO */

#ifdef DEMO

main()                          /* a small main used for demonstration  */
{
        int n;

        char *char_str();
        char *center();


        for (n = 80; n > 40; n -= 4) {
            puts(char_str(n, '.'));
            puts(center("hello world", n));
        }
}
```

```
#endif

char *char_str(length, c)         /* based on length and character, return a  */
int length;                       /*  pointer to string for use in            */
char c;                           /*  centering, offsets, etc.                */
{
        static char loc[80];              /* space enough for filled strings */
                                          /* note it is static; an auto      */
                                          /*  would evaporate upon return    */

        char *ptr = loc;                  /* make a pointer point there      */
                                          /*  as it is declared              */

        while (length--)
            *ptr++ = c;                   /* fill in the string to length    */

        *ptr = '\0';                      /* append null                     */

        return (loc);                     /* return address of string        */
}


char *center(str,width)           /* returns a pointer to the same string as  */
char *str;                        /*  passed, only centered within width      */
int width;
{
        static char buf[132];             /* location of finished string */

        char *char_str();
        char *strcpy();
        char *strcat();

        strcpy(buf, char_str((width - strlen(str)) / 2, '\040' ));

        strcat(buf, str);

        return (buf);
}
```

getnlin.c

```
/*   module title: getnlin.c
 *   function name: int getnlin()
 *
 *   author: Kim J. Brand
 *
 *   revision history:
 *       version/--date--/by reason-------------------------------------------
 *         1.0   10/01/84 kb Common C Functions initial release
 *
 *   compiled with: stdio.h
 *   compiled by:
 *
 *   linked with: void window()
 *   linked by:
 *
 *   problems:
 *
 *   description: gets a string from stdin of up to n characters and places
 *                characters at location indicated by ptr
 */

#include <stdio.h>

int getnlin(ptr,n)          /* get up to n characters from stdin, stop at   */
char *ptr;                   /* EOF or newline, put characters at pointer    */
int n;
{
        int c;                              /* all-purpose character variable */

        while ((c = getchar()) != '\n' && c != EOF && --n) {
            *ptr++ = c;
        }

        *ptr = '\0';                        /* finish with null               */

        return (c == EOF);                  /* tell parent function if program */
                                            /* aborted or reached EOF          */
}
```

gettime.c

```
/*   module title: get_time.c
 *   function names: void get_time()
 *
 *   author: Kim J. Brand
 *
 *   revision history:
 *      version/--date--/by reason------------------------------------------
 *         1.0   10/01/84 kb Common C Functions initial release
 *
 *   compiled with:
 *   compiled by:
 *
 *   linked with:
 *   linked by:
 *
 *   problems:
 *
 *   description: retrieves time and date from MS-DOS via 0x21 interrupt
 *                function call; highly DOS and compiler dependent
 */

                                /* getting the time/date from the operating */
                                /* system is an environment-dependent        */
                                /* function; here are the ways LATTICE and    */
                                /* C86 give to make direct operating          */
                                /* system calls                               */

#define C86 TRUE                      /* else program compiles for LATTICE */


#if C86                               /* C86 calls this function sysint21 */

#define intdos(x,y) sysint21(x,y)
struct _sreg {int ax,bx,cx,dx,si,di,ds,es; };

#else                                 /* LATTICE call */

struct _sreg {int ax,bx,cx,dx,si,di; };
```

```
#endif

void get_time(ptr)                      /* gets d-o-w, time/date from  */
char *ptr;                              /*   system and stores the ascii */
{                                       /*   info at ptr                */
        struct _sreg sreg;
        static char *days[ ] = {
            "Sunday",
            "Monday",
            "Tuesday",
            "Wednesday",
            "Thursday",
            "Friday",
            "Saturday"
        };
        char *dow;
        int hour;
        int minute;
        int year;
        int month;
        int day;
        char ampm;

        sreg.ax = 0x2a00;                           /* gets date from MS DOS */
        intdos(&sreg, &sreg);

        year = sreg.cx - 1900;          /* the year in two digits */
        month = sreg.dx >> 8;           /*   & the month */
        day = sreg.dx & 0xff;           /*   & date */
        dow = days[sreg.ax & 0xff];     /*   & day of week string */

        sreg.ax = 0x2c00;                           /* gets time from MS DOS */
        intdos(&sreg, &sreg);

        hour = sreg.cx >> 8;
        minute = sreg.cx & 0xff;

        if (hour >= 0 && hour <= 11)    /* converts from 24- to       */
            ampm = 'a';                 /*   12-hour format and sets */
        else                            /*   the meridian indicator   */
            ampm = 'p';

        if (hour > 12)
            hour -= 12;
        else if (hour==0)
            hour = 12;                  /* put in header */

        sprintf(ptr, "%s %02d/%02d/%02d   %02d:%02d%c",
            dow, month, day, year, hour, minute, ampm);
}
```

inchar.c

```
/*   module title: inchar.c
 *   function names: int inchar()
 *                   void outchar()
 *
 *   author: Kim J. Brand
 *
 *   revision history:
 *      version/--date--/by reason-----------------------------------------
 *        1.0   10/01/84 kb Common C Functions initial release
 *
 *   compiled with: stdio.h
 *   compiled by:
 *
 *   linked with: void amort(), kidedit(), report()
 *                int listme(), menu(), scan()
 *   linked by:
 *
 *   problems: nonportable, specifically designed for MS-DOS environment
 *             because of its use of interrupt vector call to get/send next
 *             character from/to operating system
 *
 *   description: function avoids use of standard library call so can get an
 *                unbuffered character from the operating system; this character
 *                provides instant response without entering a carriage return;
 *                inchar does not echo its character, so outchar is used
 */

#include <stdio.h>

#define C86                             /* de-comment this line if using C86 */

#ifdef C86
                                        /* LATTICE function is intdos; C86   */
#define intdos(x,y) sysint21(x,y)       /* is sysint21; use either           */
#define int86(x,y,z) sysint(x,y,z)      /* likewise for int86/sysint         */

#endif

struct _sreg {int ax,bx,cx,dx,si,di,ds,es; };

#define VIDEO_INT 0x19                  /* IBM PC uses 0x10 for              */
                                        /*  video interrupt                  */


int inchar(n)                           /* in MS DOS system, gets a          */
int n;                                  /*  character from the keyboard raw  */
{
```

```
        struct _sreg sreg;
        int c;

        sreg.ax = 0x0700;              /* get a character, wait if not ready*/
        intdos(&sreg, &sreg);          /* compiler- and DOS-dependent     */

        if (c = sreg.ax&0xff) {        /* watch out for two character-    */
           return (c);                 /* producing keystrokes            */
        }
        else {
           sreg.ax = 0x0700;
           intdos(&sreg,&sreg);
           return (sreg.ax);
        }
}

void outchar(c)                        /* send a character to the screen at  */
char c;                                /* current cursor location            */
{
        struct _sreg sreg;

        sreg.bx = 0;                   /* page 0                          */
        sreg.ax = 0x0e00 + c;          /* teletype write character command */
        int86(VIDEO_INT, &sreg, &sreg);

}
```

incharux.c

```
/*      module title: inchar.c (for unix)
 *  function names: int inchar(), outchar(), initch(), endch()
 *
 *  author: Kim J. Brand
 *
 *  revision history:
 *      version/--date--/by  reason------------------------------------------
 *        1.0  10/01/84 kb  Common C Functions initial release
 *
 *  compiled with: termio.h, fcntl.h, stdio.h
 *                 sys/types.h sys/ioctl.h for XENIX
 *  compiled by:
 *
 *  linked with:
 *  linked by:
 *
 *  problems: may only work on Unix System V, or System III with Berkeley
 *            4.2 enhancments...check your port specifications and the
 *            documentation supplied with tty(4) and ioctl(2)  (this function
 *            was designed for a MASSCOMP MC500)
 *
 *            if compiling under XENIX, include the command line argument
 *            -DXENIX when compiling this module
 *
 *  description: inchar() and outchar() are single-character, nonbuffered
 *               console read/write routines
 *               initch() must be called before using these routines
 *               endch() must be called before exiting the program
 *
 */

#include <sys/types.h>
#include <termio.h>
#include <fcntl.h>
#include <stdio.h>

#ifdef XENIX                    /* if XENIX, include ioctl header file   */
        #include <sys/ioctl.h>
#endif

static int fd;                  /* only this module knows about this fd  */
static struct termio arg;       /* used in setting and restoring terminal's */
                                /* i/o information                       */
static int c_cc4;               /* holds old value of c_cc[4], the EOF char */
```

```
int initch()                      /* called at beginning to initialize tty   */
{                                 /* properly for single char input          */

        char termname[L_ctermid];      /* array to hold term name        */
        char *ctermid();               /* ttyname function               */

        ctermid(termname);             /* gets terminal ttyname          */
        fd = open(termname, O_RDWR);   /* open the device                */

        ioctl(fd, TCGETA, &arg);

        arg.c_lflag ^= (ECHO|ICANON);  /* turns off echo and stops       */
                                       /*   translation and buffering*/
        c_cc4 = arg.c_cc[4];           /* save old value of c_cc[4] */
        arg.c_cc[4] = 1;               /* sets the number of     */
                                       /*   characters we want to one*/
        return(ioctl(fd, TCSETA, &arg));      /* return result from ioctl  */

}

int endch()                       /* called at end of routines to reset the  */
{                                 /*   tty's properly                        */

        arg.c_lflag ^= (ECHO|ICANON);  /* returned to original state   */
        arg.c_cc[4] = c_cc4;           /* restore old value of VEOF    */
        ioctl(fd, TCSETA, &arg);       /* restore old parameters       */
        close(fd);                     /* close up the file            */
        return(0);

}

int inchar()
{
        char buf[1];

        read(fd, buf, 1);

        return *buf;
}

int outchar(c)
{
        char buf[1];

        *buf = c;

        return(write(fd, buf, 1));
}
```

place.c

```
/*    module title: place.c
 *  function names: void place()
 *
 *  author: Kim J. Brand
 *
 *  revision history:
 *     version/--date--/by  reason----------------------------------------
 *        1.0   10/01/84 kb  Common C Functions initial release
 *
 *  compiled with: stdio.h
 *  compiled by:
 *
 *  linked with:
 *  linked by:
 *
 *  problems:
 *
 *  description: place() is a general-purpose cursor-positioning function
 *               that can be used with ANSI-type terminals (including the IBM
 *               PC when the ANSI.SYS file has been declared in CONFIG.SYS)
 *               and non-ANSI type terminals such as the TELEVIDEO, WYSE-50,
 *               etc. It can also be configured to operate with IBM PC-
 *               compatible systems. If it is, it uses interrupt functions to
 *               perform the cursor positioning much faster.
 */

#include <stdio.h>
#include "macros.h"              /* where we have put the definition of ROW  */
                                 /* and COL for use with ANSI, other terminals*/

#define VIDEO_INT 0x10           /* in case we use ROM-BIOS calls, we'll need */
                                 /* to know where to call it                  */

/* #define C86 */                /* C86 uses a different name for int86       */
                                 /* which is the name LATTICE uses            */
#ifdef C86                       /* provide the following macro if C86 is used*/
#define int86(x,y,z) sysint(x,y,z)
#endif


#define IBM                      /* if this line here, ROM-BIOS cursor        */
                                 /* positioning will be used                  */

#define ANSI                     /* if this line removed, the non-ANSI type   */
                                 /* cursor-positioning scheme will be used    */

#define LEAD_IN "\033="          /* for the non-ANSI terminal we want to      */
                                 /* support here, the lead-in string is an    */
                                 /* escape (0x1b) followed by an equal sign   */
```

```
void place(row, col)              /* position cursor at row and column given  */
unsigned int row;
unsigned int col;
{

#ifdef IBM                        /* compatibles only please...              */

        struct { int ax, bx, cx, dx, si, di, ds, es;  } sreg;

        sreg.ax = 0x0200;                       /* this is for positioning   */
                                                /*  the cursor               */

                                                /* remember to subtract one  */
                                                /*  because ROM-BIOS is 0,0  */
        sreg.dx = (row - 1 << 8) | col - 1;     /* set up row and column     */
        sreg.bx = 0;                            /* page number               */

        int86(VIDEO_INT, &sreg, &sreg);

#else
        int printf();

#ifdef ANSI                                     /* the ANSI sequence needs   */
        printf("\033[%d;%dH", row, col);        /*  row and column values in */
                                                /*  ascii; remember: ANSI    */
                                                /*  coordinates start at 1,1 */
#else
        printf(LEAD_IN);                        /* can't use puts cause it   */
                                                /*  adds a newline at end    */
        putchar(ROW(row));                      /* these macros just adjust  */
        putchar(COL(col));                      /*  the row/col base value to*/
                                                /*  meet the terminal's      */
#endif                                          /*  requirements             */
#endif                                          /* note nested conditionals  */
}
```

setcurs.c

```
/*    module title: set_curs.c
 *  function names: set_cursor()
 *
 *  author: Kim J. Brand
 *
 *  revision history:
 *     version/--date--/by  reason------------------------------------------
 *        1.0   10/01/84 kb  Common C Functions initial release
 *
 *  compiled with:
 *  compiled by:
 *
 *  linked with:
 *  linked by:
 *
 *  problems: IBM PC (or compatibles) only
 *
 *  description: uses the IBM PC's interrupt function calls to turn the cursor
 *               on or off, can also be used to change the shape of the cursor,
 *               as the case of it being on or off is really just a matter of
 *               defining on which raster scan line the cursor block begins;
 *               see the PC's Technical reference manual for more details
 *
 */

#include "dos.h"
#define VIDEO_INT 0x10          /* this would be 0x19 for the NEC APC III    */

#define C86                     /* C86 uses a different name for int86       */
                                /* which is the name LATTICE uses            */
#ifdef C86                      /* provide the following macro if C86 is used*/
#define int86(x,y,z) sysint(x,y,z)
#endif

void set_cursor(flag)
int flag;
{
        struct _sreg sreg;

        sreg.ax = 0x0100;
        sreg.cx = flag ? 0x0407 : 0x8000;

        int86(VIDEO_INT, &sreg, &sreg);
}
```

setmem.c

```
/*   module title: setmem.c
 *   function name: void setmem()
 *
 *   author: Kim J. Brand
 *
 *   revision history:
 *      version/--date--/by reason-------------------------------------------
 *       1.0   10/01/84 kb Common C Functions initial release
 *
 *   compiled with: stdio.h
 *   compiled by:
 *
 *   linked with: kidedit.c, numbers(), revjul(), scan(), window()
 *   linked by:
 *
 *   problems:
 *
 *   description: initializes a block of memory pointed to by addr for length
 *                given by size with val
 */


void setmem(addr, size, val)     /* fill, starting at addr, for size, with val*/
char *addr;
unsigned int size;
char val;
{
      while (size--)             /* fill up sequential bytes of memory  */
          *addr++ = val;         /*  until size counted down to zero    */

}
```

shift.c

```
/*  module title: shift.c
 *  function name: int *shl_string()
 *                 void *shr_string()
 *
 *  author: Kim J. Brand
 *
 *  revision history:
 *     version/--date--/by reason------------------------------------------------
 *        1.0   10/01/84 kb Common C Functions initial release
 *
 *  compiled with: stdio.h
 *  compiled by:
 *
 *  linked with: int scan()
 *  linked by:
 *
 *  problems:
 *
 *  description: shifts a string left and right in memory, into spaces on the
 *               left or into oblivion on the right; for left shift, if
 *               not enough room, function returns a nonzero result;
 *               fill on the right (or left) with the insert character
 *               and stop shifting when the limit character is reached
 */

#include <stdio.h>

#ifndef TRUE
#define TRUE 1
#endif

#ifndef FALSE
#define FALSE 0
#endif

int shl_string(s, insert, limit)        /* shifts string left if can into    */
char *s;                                 /*  leading spaces and returns TRUE, */
char insert;                             /*  else returns FALSE               */
char limit;
{
        char c;

        if (*s++ != ' ')                /* for shift left, must be at    */
            return FALSE ;              /*  least one space on the left  */

        while ((c = *s) != limit) {     /* as long as do not             */
            *(s - 1) = c;               /*  reach limit character, move  */
            s++;                        /*  the character left one step  */
        }
```

```
        *(s - 1) = insert;                     /* slip in the insert character now  */
                                               /*   that there's room               */
        return TRUE ;
}


void shr_string(s, limit)                      /* pass a pointer to the original    */
char *s;                                       /*   string; limit can be flag       */
char limit;                                    /*   character or end-of-string null */
{
        char c;                                /* an all-purpose character variable */
        char temp = ' ';                       /*   initialized with space; fill    */
                                               /*   character later used to move    */
                                               /*   characters found                */

        while ((c = *s++) != limit) {
            *(s - 1) = temp;
            temp = c;
        }
}
```

sindex.c

```
/*    module title: sindex.c
 *  function names: int sindex()
 *
 *  author: Kim J. Brand
 *
 *  revision history:
 *     version/--date--/by  reason------------------------------------------
 *        1.0  10/01/84 kb  Common C Functions initial release
 *
 *  compiled with:
 *  compiled by:
 *
 *  linked with: int scan()
 *  linked by:
 *
 *  problems:
 *
 *  description: returns the integer location of a given character in the
 *               string argument or -1 if the character is not found.
 *
 */

int sindex(ptr,c)                /* locate the position of a specified    */
char *ptr;                       /*  character inside a string            */
int c;
{
        int n = 0;
        int length;

        length = strlen(ptr);           /* find length of string         */

        while (*ptr != c && *ptr++)
           n++;

        return ((length == n) ? -1 : n);
}
```

Function Group Four: Runable Programs

module:	function:
kidedit.c	main()

module:	functions:
amort.c	main() int amort()

module:	function:
pipe.c	main()

module:	functions:
list.c	main() void banner()

These final modules are really programs that you may find useful to enter and enjoyable to run. Given your newly obtained skill in C programming, they should present some interesting opportunities for modification or enhancement.

kidedit.c

This little program demonstrates some simple flow control concepts and gives the kids something fun and reasonably harmless to do with your computer.

Most children usually want to type on the screen and get the printer to make a copy of what they type. One solution is to redirect the console to the list device, but that isn't flashy enough, nor does the approach let the children correct their mistakes. Putting the terminal in half-duplex mode will work but won't allow what is created on the screen to be printed. With the program presented here, a child can write on the screen, create simple character figures, get a "printout," and then start over or add to it if they want.

Other than the command to position the cursor at its home position, the only other cursor control features required are up, down, left and right. A box is drawn that defines the drawing area, and the cursor is kept in it. Ctrl-P is defined to send the drawing to the printer, and the Escape key is defined to clear the screen and paint a new box. These may be changed to suit your tastes as desired.

Once again, it is necessary to go directly to the source (the operating system) for the input characters. Some compilers may want to return certain key sequences as their multiple key ASCII equivalents (for example, the cursor positioning keys), and may not want to return some keys at all (for example, the Escape key). Although such problems detract from portability, a variety of methods are available to get "raw" input from stdin. In this case, we need to let the program decide when to echo characters and when to get characters without having to see a carriage return.

kidedit.c

```
/*  module title: kidedit.c
 *  function name: main()
 *
 *  author: Kim J. Brand
 *
 *  revision history:
 *     version/--date--/by reason---------------------------------------------
 *        1.0   10/01/84 kb Common C Functions initial release
 *
 *  compiled with: stdio.h, ctype.h
 *  compiled by:
 *
 *  linked with: int inchar()
 *               void say();
 *  linked by:
 *
 *  problems:
 *
 *  description: a simple screen editor for kids; displays only one
 *               screenful, provides a border within which the cursor is
 *               trapped, prints the window when ctrl-P is pressed, and
 *               clears the window when escape is pressed
 *
 */

#include <stdio.h>
#include <ctype.h>

#define CLS "\033[2J"                    /* ANSI clear string             */

#define UP_ARROW 1864                    /* values returned from the      */
#define DOWN_ARROW 1872                  /*  cursor-positioning arrows    */
#define LEFT_ARROW 1867                  /*   on the IBM PC and NEC APC-III */
#define RIGHT_ARROW 1869

#define DOWN "\033[1B"                   /* strings to move cursor around */
#define UP "\033[1A"                     /* again, ANSI escape sequences  */
#define LEFT "\033[1D"
#define RIGHT "\033[1C"
#define HOME "\033[1;1H"

#define CR '\r'
#define SPACE '\040'

#define NORTH 5                          /* define size of window by      */
#define SOUTH 18                         /*  its line and column borders  */
#define EAST 60
#define WEST 20
```

```
#define PRINT 0x10                    /* ctrl-P to print              */
#define CLEAR 0x1b                    /* escape to clear screen       */
#define CNTRL_C 0x3                   /* ctrl-C to stop               */

char screen[SOUTH+1][EAST+2];         /* location of screen;          */
                                      /* extra position on right      */
                                      /*  is where indefectible string */
                                      /*  end null is kept; null is   */
                                      /*  there because this extern array */
                                      /*  is cleared to spaces at the start*/
main()
{
        int n;
        int c;
        int horizontal;                        /* location in screen array */
        int vertical;
        FILE *fp;

        FILE *fopen();
        int inchar();
        void say();
        void setmem();

        fp = fopen("PRN", "w");
        if (!fp) {
            say("Can't seem to talk to the printer...\n");
            exit(1);
        }

        goto clear;                            /* clear screen and        */
                                               /*  initialize array to    */
                                               /*  spaces at the start,   */
                                               /*  then rejoin the while, */
                                               /*  which is in progress   */
        while ((c = inchar()) != EOF) {

            switch (c) {

                case UP_ARROW:
                    if (--vertical < NORTH + 1) {
                        vertical = NORTH + 1;
                        break;
                    }
                    say(UP);
                    break;
```

```
                case DOWN_ARROW:
down:               if (++vertical > SOUTH - 1) {
                        vertical = SOUTH - 1;
                        break;
                    }
                    say(DOWN);
                    break;

                case LEFT_ARROW:
                    if (--horizontal < WEST + 1) {
                        horizontal = WEST + 1;
                        break;
                    }
                    say(LEFT);
                    break;

                case PRINT:
                    for (n = 0; n <= SOUTH; n++) {
                        fputs(screen[n], fp);
                        putc('\n', fp);
                    }
                    break;

                case CR:
                    horizontal = 0;                     /* go west, young man! */
                    putchar(c);
                    for (; horizontal < WEST + 1; horizontal++)
                        say(RIGHT);
                    c = DOWN_ARROW;
                    goto down;
                    break;

                case CLEAR:
                                                    /* clear screen and draw   */
                                                    /* zigzag box on screen    */

clear:              say(CLS);

                    for (n = 0; n <= SOUTH; n++)                 /* fill array */
                        setmem(screen[n], EAST + 1, SPACE);  /*  with spaces*/

                                                    /* go down to top   */
                                                    /* of box           */

                    for (vertical = 0; vertical < NORTH; vertical++)
                        say(DOWN);                  /* move to left edge */

                    for (horizontal = 0; horizontal < WEST; horizontal++)
                        say(RIGHT);                 /* mark top of box   */
```

```
        for (; horizontal <= EAST; horizontal++) {
            putchar('-');
            screen[vertical][horizontal] = '-';
        }

        putchar(CR), horizontal = 0;            /* back to left    */
        say(DOWN), vertical++;                  /* and down one    */
                                                /* over to left edge*/
        for (; horizontal < WEST; horizontal++)
            say(RIGHT);

                            /* now draw left and right edges for */
                            /* height-1 lines, zigzag fashion    */

        for (; vertical < SOUTH; vertical++) {
            putchar('|'), screen[vertical][horizontal++] = '|';

            for (; horizontal < EAST; horizontal++)
                say(RIGHT);

            putchar('|'), screen[vertical][horizontal++] = '|';

            for (; horizontal > WEST; horizontal--)
                say(LEFT);

            say(DOWN);
        }
                                        /* draw the bottom line   */
        putchar(CR), horizontal = 0;

        for (; horizontal < WEST; horizontal++)
            say(RIGHT);

        for (; horizontal <= EAST; horizontal++) {
            putchar('-');
            screen[vertical][horizontal] = '-';
        }

        say(HOME);                              /* home the cursor   */

        for (vertical = 0; vertical < NORTH + 1; vertical++)
            say(DOWN);                          /* move to left edge */
        for (horizontal = 0; horizontal < WEST + 1; horizontal++)
            say(RIGHT);

        break;

    default:
```

```
                if (!isprint(c) || horizontal == EAST)
                    continue;                  /* don't want any other ctrl */
                                               /*  characters here (or del), */
                                               /*  also prevents             */
                                               /*  putting character on      */
                                               /*  top of the border         */

                screen[vertical][horizontal] = c;   /* put c there */
                putchar(c);
                                               /* advance indexes to    */
                                               /*  right after char sent */
                                               /*  by falling into RIGHT */

            case RIGHT_ARROW:
                if (++horizontal > EAST) {
                    horizontal = EAST;
                    continue;
                }
                if (c == RIGHT_ARROW)          /* could get here by      */
                    say(RIGHT);                /*  falling through from  */
                                               /*  the default           */

                break;

        } /* end of switch */

        fflush(fp);
        fflush(stdout);

    } /* end of while */
}
```

amort.c

This function produces an amortization table on either the screen or the printer, given parameters for the payment per period, principal amount, interest per period, number of periods, period number at which to start the report, and I/O device to send the table to. A small main is included that prompts for these amounts and invokes the function.

The program demonstrates the ability of C to redirect its output to either the terminal or the printer device, given only a pointer to an I/O structure.

Two nonstandard library functions are used: center() and inchar().

center() centers the report title inside a field that is 56 characters wide. The function actually just pads the front of the string (within a static array) with spaces and returns a pointer to this new string for use with the printing function.

inchar() is an operating-system and compiler-dependent function that retrieves a single character from the console without requiring the use of a carriage return. The function operates outside of C's normally buffered I/O facilities, which rely on some end-of-block marker (like a carriage return) to signal the end of input and the need to transfer to the parent function what has been received.

This feature necessitates the use of the fflush() call after the line prompting the user for input to get the next screenful of data. Without using fflush(), the data on the screen might not include the last several characters output by the function. Such characters would still be in the output buffer, waiting for a newline to signal that the block was complete.

Many environments make use of another function, ioctrl(), to select a "raw" mode that can force the I/O functions to work one character at a time. Although this function may give more desirable results for I/O to your video terminal, just about all other I/O devices are better operated in buffered mode.

Sample execution:

```
Enter the number of periods --> 120

Enter the payment per period --> 300

Enter the principal amount --> 10000

Enter the Periodic Interest Rate --> .01

Enter the starting period --> 1

Send output to console (0) or printer (1) --> 1
```

Sample output:

```
Enter the number of periods --> 120
Enter the payment per period --> 300
Enter the principal amount --> 10000
Enter the periodic interest rate --> .01
Enter the starting period --> 1
Send output to console (0) or printer (1) --> 0
```

```
                  Loan Amortization Table


            Payment per period = $      300.00
            Number of periods  =           120
            Principal amount   = $   10000.00
            Periodic interest  =        0.0100
            Starting period    =             1


                      Appl'd to          Prnc'pl   Accum
        Period  Payment  Principal  Interest  Balance  Interest

          1    300.00    200.00    100.00   9800.00   100.00
          2    300.00    202.00     98.00   9598.00   198.00
          3    300.00    204.02     95.98   9393.98   293.98
          4    300.00    206.06     93.94   9187.92   387.92
          5    300.00    208.12     91.88   8979.80   479.80
          6    300.00    210.20     89.80   8769.60   569.60
          7    300.00    212.30     87.70   8557.29   657.29
          8    300.00    214.43     85.57   8342.87   742.87
          9    300.00    216.57     83.43   8126.29   826.29
         10    300.00    218.74     81.26   7907.56   907.56
         11    300.00    220.92     79.08   7686.63   986.63
```

Press return to continue...

Period	Payment	Appl'd to Principal	Interest	Prnc'pl Balance	Accum Interest
12	300.00	223.13	76.87	7463.50	1063.50
13	300.00	225.37	74.63	7238.13	1138.13
14	300.00	227.62	72.38	7010.52	1210.52
15	300.00	229.89	70.11	6780.62	1280.62
16	300.00	232.19	67.81	6548.43	1348.43
17	300.00	234.52	65.48	6313.91	1413.91
18	300.00	236.86	63.14	6077.05	1477.05
19	300.00	239.23	60.77	5837.82	1537.82
20	300.00	241.62	58.38	5596.20	1596.20
21	300.00	244.04	55.96	5352.16	1652.16
22	300.00	246.48	53.52	5105.68	1705.68
23	300.00	248.94	51.06	4856.74	1756.74
24	300.00	251.43	48.57	4605.31	1805.31
25	300.00	253.95	46.05	4351.36	1851.36
26	300.00	256.49	43.51	4094.87	1894.87
27	300.00	259.05	40.95	3835.82	1935.82
28	300.00	261.64	38.36	3574.18	1974.18
29	300.00	264.26	35.74	3309.92	2009.92
30	300.00	266.90	33.10	3043.02	2043.02
31	300.00	269.57	30.43	2773.45	2073.45

Press return to continue...

Period	Payment	Appl'd to Principal	Interest	Prnc'pl Balance	Accum Interest
32	300.00	272.27	27.73	2501.19	2101.19
33	300.00	274.99	25.01	2226.20	2126.20
34	300.00	277.74	22.26	1948.46	2148.46
35	300.00	280.52	19.48	1667.94	2167.94
36	300.00	283.32	16.68	1384.62	2184.62
37	300.00	286.15	13.85	1098.47	2198.47
38	300.00	289.02	10.98	809.46	2209.46
39	300.00	291.91	8.09	517.55	2217.55
40	300.00	294.82	5.18	222.73	2222.73
41	224.95	222.73	2.23	0.00	2224.95

Press return to continue...

amort.c

```
/*  module title: amort.c
 *  function names: void amort()
 *                  main() for demo
 *
 *  author: Kim J. Brand
 *
 *  revision history:
 *    version/--date--/by reason------------------------------------------
 *       1.0   10/01/84 kb Common C Functions initial release
 *
 *  compiled with: stdio.h
 *  compiled by:
 *
 *  linked with: int inchar()
 *               char *center()
 *  linked by:
 *
 *  problems:   reformatting of output is required for amounts over
 *              $999999.99 because float field width is specified as %9.2
 *
 *  description: amortizes a principal amount over the number of periods
 *               specified at a periodic interest rate (the interest
 *               rate charged per period); sends output to console or
 *               printer; sends form feeds if printer and pauses at each
 *               page if console
 */

#include <stdio.h>

#define PRNTR_PAGE 56          /* leaves room for the MARGIN           */
#define CONSOLE_PAGE 19
#define EJECT '\f'             /* may be printer dependent             */
#define START 9               /* number of line from top of page at   */
                              /* which to start                       */
#define MARGIN 5              /*  top and bottom margins               */

#define DEMO

#ifdef DEMO
                              /* demonstration main for amort()        */
main()                        /* this main sets up the number of       */
{                             /* periods, payment per each, principal, */
        double pmt_period;    /* periodic interest rate, and starting  */
        int no_periods;       /* period for the report (does not have to */
        double principal;     /* be the first)                         */
```

```
        double ppr;              /* periodic percentage rate: the interest  */
                                 /*   charged per each period               */
    int start_period;
    int io_device;              /* user selects console or printer          */

    void amort();

    /* watch out for some compilers that do not flush non-newline   */
    /* terminated string to the screen; you may need to add fflush()s */
    /* after the printf()s if this happens                          */

    printf("\nEnter the number of periods --> ");
    scanf("%d", &no_periods);

    printf("\nEnter the payment per period --> ");
    scanf("%lf", &pmt_period);

    printf("\nEnter the principal amount --> ");
    scanf("%lf", &principal);

    printf("\nEnter the periodic interest rate --> ");
    scanf("%lf", &ppr);

    printf("\nEnter the starting period --> ");
    scanf("%d", &start_period);

    printf("\nSend output to console (0) or printer (1) --> ");
    scanf("%d", &io_device);

                                        /* let amort function do */
                                        /*  all the work         */

    amort(pmt_period, no_periods, principal, ppr, start_period, io_device);

}

#endif


void amort(pmt_period, no_periods, principal, ppr, start_period, io_device)
double pmt_period;
int no_periods;
double principal;
double ppr;
int start_period;
int io_device;
{
```

```
      int pmt;                          /* a temporary payment number     */
      double interest;                  /* periodic interest              */
      double amortized;                 /* amount of the loan amortized   */
                                        /*  per each payment              */
      int pmt_no = start_period;        /* payment to start with          */
      double balance = principal;       /* what is left                   */
      double tot_interest = 0.0;        /* accumulated interest           */
      int lines = START;                /* number of lines used up with   */
                                        /*  heading before first line     */
                                        /*  of calculated report          */
      FILE *fp;                         /* I/O stream where output goes    */

      FILE *fopen();
      char *center();

      if (io_device)                    /* these special file names do not */
          fp = fopen("PRN", "w");       /*  cause file to be created, just */
      else                              /*  I/O channel to be opened       */
          fp = stdout;

      if (io_device)                    /* you may want to check for failure */
          fputc(EJECT, fp);             /* start new page                 */

      fprintf(fp, "\n%s\n", center("Loan Amortization Table",56));

      fprintf(fp, "\n\t     Payment per Period = $%10.2f", pmt_period);
      fprintf(fp, "\n\t     Number of Periods  = %10d", no_periods);
      fprintf(fp, "\n\t     Principal Amount   = $%10.2f", principal);
      fprintf(fp, "\n\t     Periodic Interest  = %10.4f", ppr);
      fprintf(fp, "\n\t     Starting Period    = %10d\n", start_period);

      /* figure where we are in amortization table based on when we were  */
      /* told to start displaying the figures                            */

      for(pmt = 1; pmt < pmt_no; pmt++) {
          tot_interest += (interest = balance * ppr);
          balance -= pmt_period - interest;
      }

      while (balance != 0) {            /* loop continues until the       */
                                        /*  balance due is calculated     */
                                        /*  to be or set to zero, when    */
                                        /*  no_periods is counted down to 0 */

                                        /* print header                   */
  fprintf(fp, "\n                     Appl'd to           Prnc'pl   Accum");
  fprintf(fp, "\n Period  Payment  Principal  Interest   Balance  Interest\n\n")
```

```
        do {                        /* do for each line on the page up       */
                                    /*  to the max on the page, then start over */
                                    /*  by printing a form feed and a new heading*/
                                    /*  by escaping to the outer while        */

            tot_interest += (interest = balance * ppr);

            amortized = pmt_period - interest;

            if (balance - amortized < 0 || pmt_no == no_periods) {
                pmt_period = balance + interest;
                amortized = balance;
                balance = 0;
            }
            else
                balance -= amortized;
                                            /* print all data here       */
            fprintf(fp, " %5d", pmt_no);
            fprintf(fp, " %9.2f  %9.2f %9.2f %9.2f %9.2f\n",
                    pmt_period, amortized, interest, balance, tot_interest);

            ++pmt_no;                       /* increment payment number  */

        } while (lines++ < (io_device ? PRNTR_PAGE-MARGIN : CONSOLE_PAGE)
                    && balance != 0);

        if(io_device)
            fputc(EJECT, fp);
        else {
            fprintf(fp, "\nPress return to continue...");
            fflush(fp);                     /* ensure message prints     */
            inchar();                       /* just want to stop         */
                                            /*  until a key is pressed,  */
                                            /*  then erase the line      */
            printf("\r              \n");
        }

        if(io_device)
            for (lines = 0; lines < MARGIN; lines++)/* offset from       */
                fputc('\n', fp);                    /*   the bottom      */
        else
            lines = 0;

    } /* end of while on number of periods */

    fclose(fp);

}
```

pipe.c

This short program actually hides a good deal of power in its 20 lines. The program is included to demonstrate two features of C programs. First, pipe. c shows the use of command line arguments to pass parameters to a program. Second, the program makes use of I/O streams that are opened automatically at the start of each program.

In the program, argc is checked for a value greater than two. If the value is greater, a friendly reminder about how the program is supposed to be used is printed. The same message will be printed if a question mark is supplied as the first (and most likely the only) character of the second command line argument. (Remember that the program name itself counts as one.) Finally, if there are only two arguments and the first character of the second argument is not a hyphen, the program aborts with the reminder. Notice the I/O stream to which the reminder is sent: stderr. This feature is subtle but important.

The purpose of this program is to copy its input to its output. In the typical case, stdin and stdout will both be assigned to files. Under MS-DOS, the command line will look like this:

```
A>pipe <infile >outfile
```

This line has the effect of redirecting stdin to infile and stdout to outfile. In every other case in this book, stdout is assumed to be the user console; therefore, functions like putc() and printf() are assumed to send their output there. In this case, however, it is highly likely that stdout will be redirected to a file, or even to the printer (by >prn:). The method provided by the operating system (and C) to send error messages (and the like) to the user, even if stdout has been redirected somewhere else, is to define the I/O stream stderr to point always to the console. This method is used here.

If the b flag is used on the command line, each character read from stdin is AND'ed with 0x7f, thus effectively resetting any high bits. This function will be valuable to those who try to type out a file edited with one of the word processors that set this bit to signal special features to their companion printing programs.

You may also use this program to strip the high bits of files that are being printed by the program list found elsewhere in this book.

For more information on piping and redirection, you should refer to your compiler and operating system manuals.

pipe.c

```
/*   module title: pipe.c
 *   function name: main() for demo
 *
 *   author: Kim J. Brand
 *
 *   revision history:
 *      version/--date--/by  reason------------------------------------------
 *        1.0   10/01/84 kb  Common C Functions initial release
 *
 *   compiled with: stdio.h
 *   compiled by:
 *
 *   linked with:
 *   linked by:
 *
 *   problems:
 *
 *   description: just echos stdin to stdout; in an MS-DOS/UNIX environment the
 *                command line can define source and destination streams; if
 *                the flag '-b' is included on the command line, bit seven
 *                of each character is reset
 */

#include <stdio.h>

main(argc,argv)                     /* only a demonstation program           */
int argc;                           /* command line arguments supplied       */
char *argv[];                       /* array of pointers to the words there   */
{
        int c;                      /* the character that gets moved in/out   */
        char flag;

        if (argc > 2 || *argv[1] == '?' || (argc == 2 && *argv[1] != '-')) {
            fputs("Usage: pipe <source >destination [-b]\n", stderr);
            fputs("  the -b flag strips high bits during transfer", stderr);
            exit(1);
        }

        flag = (*(++argv[1]) == 'b' ? 0x7f : 0xff);

        while ((c = getc(stdin)) != EOF)        /* until we see end of file  */
            putc(c & flag, stdout);             /*  just keep copying        */

}
```

list.c

This program is quite valuable as a listing utility for program source code. The program includes only one option: adding line numbers to the listing output. In the pattern of many UNIX-style utilities, list.c will abort after showing you its proper invocation parameters.

These parameters are

```
list [-n] file [file [file [... ]]]
```

You can therefore get list.c to print one or more files simply by typing their names on the command line after the list. By including the optional flag -n somewhere within this list, the file names that follow will be listed, including line numbers.

A feature of list.c that I've never seen in another listing program is the placement of a file name + time/date + page number banner at the top *and* bottom of each listing page. After accumulating reams of listings in binders, you, too, will experience the inconvenience of turning pages over or prying up bindings, then finding banners listed at only the tops of pages.

This program demonstrates the use of the argument count and vectors associated with the main() function, as well as output to the list device. The program makes use of a banner() function to format the string printed at the tops and bottoms of the listing pages. static variable arrays and nested control structures are used throughout.

In addition, the program demonstrates the use of operating-system and environment-dependent functions to retrieve the system time/date. The banner is constructed only once at the beginning of the listing for each file. Only then is the time and date queried. On subsequent pages, only the page number is added.

list.c

```
/*   module title: list.c
 *   function names: main()
 *                   void banner()
 *
 *   author: Kim J. Brand
 *
 *   revision history:
 *      version/--date--/by reason------------------------------------------
 *        1.0   10/01/84 kb Common C Functions initial release
 *
 *   compiled with: stdio.h
 *   compiled by:
 *
 *   linked with: void get_time()
 *   linked by:
 *
 *   problems: if line numbers are requested, program will always indicate
 *             one more line than really exists in the file because the line
 *             number is printed before the next character is retrieved
 *             from the file
 *
 *   description: This print utility for source code prints a banner at the top
 *                and bottom of a page, which can be seen after the listing
 *                has been bound. Optional line numbers can be printed, but
 *                the maximum line number provided for (by virtue of its print
 *                spec: '%4d') is 9999.
 */

#include <stdio.h>

#ifndef TRUE
#define TRUE 1
#endif

#ifndef FALSE
#define FALSE 0
#endif

FILE *fp_out;                           /* need this (printer) to be    */
                                        /* usable throughout the module */
main(argc,argv)
int argc;
char *argv[];
{
                                        /* tab locations */
    static int tab[] = {
        8, 16, 24, 32, 40, 48, 56, 64, 72, 80, 88, 96, 104, 112, 120, 128
    };
```

```
int c;
int i;
int lines;                       /* TRUE means you want line numbers */
int page;
int on_line;                     /* line you are on        */
int on_page;                     /* page you are on        */
int on_char;                     /* character you are on */
int to_col;
FILE *fp_in;

FILE *fopen();
void banner();

if (argc < 2) {
    printf("list: usage: list [-n] filename [filename [filename [...]]]\n");
    exit(0);
}

if (!(fp_out = fopen("PRN", "w"))) {
    printf("list: can't open printer stream\n");
    exit(1);
}

lines = FALSE;                   /* assume do not want line numbers */

for (i = 1; i < argc; i++) {

    if (argv[i][0] == '-') {     /* have a flag?           */
        if (argv[i][1] == 'n')
          ` lines = TRUE;        /* if right, set up       */
        continue;                /*  test variable         */
    }

    fp_in = fopen(argv[i], "r");
    if (!fp_in) {
        printf("list: %s can't be opened\n", argv[i]);
        continue;
    }

    on_line = 1;                 /* reset variables for this file */
    page = 1;

    putc('\f', fp_out);
    banner(1, argv[i], page);    /* first call to banner sets the */

    on_page = 4;                 /*  time for entire listing      */
    on_char = 0;

    if (lines)
        fprintf(fp_out, "%4d: ", on_line);
```

```
        while ((c = getc(fp_in)) != EOF) {
            if (c == '\t') {                      /* moving sideways with a tab */
                to_col = tab[on_char / 8];
                while (to_col - on_char) {
                    putc(' ', fp_out);
                    on_char++;
                }
            }
            else {                          /* moving down with \n or \f       */
                if (c == '\f') {         /*  or a regular character            */
                    while (++on_page < 58)
                        putc('\n', fp_out);
                }
                else {
                    if (c == '\n') {
                        on_char = 0;
                        on_page++;
                        on_line++;
                        putc(c, fp_out);
                                                        /* set up next line */
                        if (lines && on_page != 58)     /* if on this page */
                            fprintf(fp_out, "%4d: ", on_line);
                    }
                    else {
                        putc(c, fp_out);
                        on_char++;
                    }
                }
                if (on_page == 58) {              /* if we reach bottom,       */
                    fputs("\n\n", fp_out);       /*  divide text from banner, */
                    banner(0, argv[i], page++);  /*  print banner; this       */
                    putc('\f', fp_out);          /*  argv parameter just takes*/
                    banner(0, argv[i], page);    /*  up space                 */
                    if (lines)
                        fprintf(fp_out, "%4d: ", on_line);
                    on_page = 4;
                    on_char = 0;
                }
            }
        }
        while (++on_page < 61)
            putc('\n', fp_out);
        banner(0, argv[i], page);
    }
}
```

```
void banner(flag, name, page)        /* print banner at fp_out including time,    */
int flag;                            /*   date, file name, and page number; fix   */
char *name;                          /*   time at call flag when <> 0             */
int page;
{
        static char header[80];              /* space for header */
        static char time[40];                /* space for time/date */
        void get_time();                     /* puts d-o-w, time/date at point-*/
                                             /*   er where it is passed points */
        if (flag) {
            get_time(time);
            sprintf(header, ">>>> %s   %s   page: ", name, time);
        }
        fprintf(fp_out, header);
        fprintf(fp_out, "%03d\n\n", page);

}
```

Appendix A

Glossary

Aggregate—A data type formed from a combination of simple types. Some aggregates are formed by combining other aggregates. For example, `int scores[];` defines an aggregate of `int`s combined to form an array.

Compile time—Refers to actions taken by the compiler during its translation of the program's source code into assembly language or an object module. Typically, a distinction is drawn between actions taken at compile time and actions that occur during run time.

Compiler switches—Included in the operation protocol of C compilers to allow the user to select or deselect features that are optional. For example, compilers used to generate programs for the 8088/86 offer a choice among two or more memory models that allow the production of smaller/faster programs if the memory space required is under 64K. The compiler has to be told whether one of these models is desired; a switch given in the command that starts the compiler is a convenient method to use.

Constant expression—One that has a value known at compile time.

Define—As used in this text, to define a variable includes making a place for it in memory and optionally giving the variable a value. External storage class variables are said to be defined so long as they are not declared with the keyword `extern`. Statics are automatically defined by their declaration. Both these storage classes are initialized to zero by default unless specifically initialized to another value in their declarations.

External storage class—Obtained by a variable (or function) by its being declared outside a function. Externals are automatically zeroed prior to the start of the program.

File I/O—In C, file I/O may mean more than reading and writing to disk files. In particular, such actions are considered to take place on "streams" that may be "redirected" by the operating system at run time. In other words, file I/O includes communication with the user's console, one or more real disk files, or any other device; the program really can't (and shouldn't be able to) tell the difference.

Flow control—As used in this text, flow control describes those statements of the C language that affect the sequential execution of program statements found in the source code.

Index—Used to reference an element of an array variable. The element may be the simple data type that is stored there, for example, cards[1][1], which retrieves an int. When the number of indexes supplied does not completely specify the elemental address, the address of a region within the array is calculated and treated as a constant. (In other words, no memory is allocated for storage of the value; storage would be allocated in the case of a variable.)

Indirection—Access of data through a pointer or pointers. C is known for its reliance on pointers to give access to data structures through a variable that holds the data's address in memory.

I/O redirection—The I/O scheme that allows a program access to I/O devices by means of an indexed reference into an array of structures. When a C program requests I/O services from the operating system at run time, the program supplies an index into an array of structures constructed to manage the particular details pertinent to the I/O channels available. Independent of the running program, the elements of this array, each defining an I/O protocol, can be changed. Because the running program only knows how to access I/O channels by their index in this array, changing the contents of an array element is transparent to the program and provides C programs with the ability to decide where program input and output come from/go to at run time.

Keyword—A word that has an intrinsic meaning to the C compiler and may not be used as an identifier. C keywords are listed in Appendix B.

Library—A file in which separately compiled modules are concatenated in their object module formats. During the link phase of a program's development into an executable form, the linker will search one or more libraries for routines referenced in the other object modules. Improved performance (due to a single file reference) and simpler operation (due to the collection of many routines in one place) are the rationale for using a library.

Linking—The process of linking one or more object modules together with one or more libraries accomplishes two purposes: (1) the modules can reference functions that have been separately compiled apart from the source of the original module by making "links" between the parent and child functions; and (2) the object module format produced as output from the compiler or assembler is converted into an executable format (and possibly relocatable at run time) compatible with the operating system loader.

Object module format—All relocating assemblers and most compilers produce their output in object modules that are formatted according to the requirements of the linker and/or operating system to be used. This format details the attributes of the variables and functions used by and shared within the program, and also indicates where certain parts of the program are located in the processor's address space when the program is executed. (See Relocatable object code.)

Recursion—The ability of a program to call itself. Recursion pertains to the way in which variables used by the function are created. A recursive function creates an independent set of auto variables with each entry. In this way, variables that were being used in the function before it called itself are preserved in the next (and possibly further) passes through the same code; variables are not "overlaid."

Reentrancy—A function's capacity to be executed simultaneously by different processes. Functions that exist in an interrupt-driven environment must sometimes be able to be invoked by two different tasks, where one task may start a function before another task's use of the same function is completed. Variables must be kept separate, and results must be returned to the right place. Reentrant functions are always capable of being recursive; the converse is not always true.

Relocatable object code—The object module format produced by relocating assemblers and most compilers. This code does not typically include absolute address references. Instead, all addresses required to be known before the program can run are relative and are determined later, usually by the linker, by adjustment of a base address. In this way, separately compiled modules may be linked as required and, when necessary, without the entire source code being processed for each new application.

Spatial performance—A measure of a program's economy in its use of main memory. Compilers that produce smaller programs are usually more desirable than compilers that use memory less efficiently. Spatial performance is sometimes considered together with temporal performance in rating compilers.

Temporal performance—A measure of the time required for code generated by a compiler to execute a given algorithm. Different compilers sometimes produce quite different results in speed comparisons of the code they generate from identical source code. Temporal performance is most often considered together with spatial performance in rating compilers.

White space—Generally disregarded in C program source code and typically ignored within formatted numeric strings. White space generally consists of the ASCII space (0x20), tab (0x09), and newline (0x0a) characters.

Appendix B

C Reserved Words

auto	double	if	sizeof
break	else	int	static
case	entry	long	struct
char	enum	register	switch
continue	extern	typedef	union
default	float	return	unsigned
do	for	short	while
	goto		void

Possibly:

    asm
    fortran

Appendix C

Summary of Functions

Functions indicated by a right triangle (▶) are from a *real* "standard library." Others have been created in this book.

```
char *adv(ptr)
        char *ptr;
```

Advances a pointer from (presumably) the beginning of a string past any leading white space to the first non-white-space character. Used in scan() to create a suitable pointer to pass to atof(), which in some implementations cannot handle leading white space.

Note: The line beginning with void amort should appear as one line but due to space restrictions appears as two lines in text.

```
void amort(pmt_period, no_periods, principal, ppr,
        start_period, io_device)
        double pmt_period;
        int no_periods;
        double principal;
        double ppr;
        int start_period;
        int io_device;
```

Prepares an amortization table, given parameters as shown on either the user console or the list device.

```
▶double atof(ptr)
        char *ptr;
```

Returns a double converted from the ASCII string at pointer. Note that the use of atof() should probably be discouraged in favor of sscanf(), which allows more control over the conversion. atof()'s use was justified in scan() for performance reasons. The System

V function double strtod() performs the same function but with more control over failure and results.

▶int atoi(ptr)
        char *ptr;

Converts the string at ptr into the integer returned from the function. The System V function long strtol(), which returns a long, is equivalent [as is long atol()] so long as the results were cast to int.

▶long atol(ptr)
        char *ptr;

Converts the string at ptr into the long integer returned from the function. See int atoi() for more details regarding the System V equivalent.

void banner(flag, name, page)
        int flag;
        char *name;
        int page;

Creates for the list() function a page header that includes the file name (from name) and the page number (from page). If flag is non-zero, banner() uses get_time() to initialize an internal static buffer with the current system time and date. Thereafter, for succeeding calls to banner() with flag equal to zero, the header is built with only the page number changing.

▶bdos(fcode, dx)
        int fcode;
        unsigned dx;

This function is usable primarily in PC DOS/MS-DOS environments to access an operating system function through the 0x21 entry point. The value placed in fcode determines the function to be performed, whereas the value in dx is passed to the function in the 8088/8086 DX register.

void blank(row, col, width)
        int row;
        int col;
        int width;

Fills a row on the console with spaces from `row, col` to the end of the line. Note that a `#define` in the module allows use with ANSI and non-ANSI terminals.

```
void bump()
```

Moves the cursor forward one position. Used in `scan()`.

```
▶char *calloc(number, size)
      unsigned int number;
      unsigned int size;
```

Returns a pointer to an area of memory `number * size` big, or else zero. The function zeros the space for you automatically and is used in combination with `free`, which gives back memory to the operating system.

```
char *center(ptr, width)
      char *ptr;
      int width;
```

Returns a pointer to a `static` string that has been constructed with the string from `ptr` placed in it; the string is centered in a space `width` characters wide.

```
char *char_str(length, c)
      int length;
      char c;
```

Returns a pointer to a character string `length` characters long and filled with character `c`.

```
int compare_mask(test, given)
      char *test;
      char *given;
```

Compares the characters in the `mask` string at `test` with characters found in string at `given` to see whether invalid characters have been entered. Used in the module `scan.c`.

```
int display(str, n, hv)
      char *str[ ];
      int n;
      int hv;
```

Displays n menu choices in the array str[ ] horizontally or vertically, as determined by hv on the user's console. Returns -1 or the number of the menu item selected.

```
▶void exit(status)
      int status;
```

Terminates the program that calls exit() and passes the value status back to the operating system or parent process that called the program. In some cases, the action of exit() closes any open files, but this varies from library to library and should not be relied on.

```
▶int fclose(fp)
      FILE *fp;
```

Closes the file associated with the file pointer fp.

```
void fill(addr, size, val)
      char *addr;
      unsigned int size;
      char val;
```

For length size, fills the memory area pointed to by addr with the character val.

```
▶int fflush(fp)
      FILE *fp;
```

Empties the I/O buffer associated with fp. This function is useful when your idea of when to flush open buffers differs from that of the operating system, particularly when writing lines not terminated with \n to the user console or other devices.

```
▶char *fgets(ptr, length, fp)
      char *ptr;
      int length;
      FILE *fp;
```

Reads up to length - 1 characters to ptr from fp and returns a pointer to the null-terminated string (a copy of ptr) if successful, or else null.

```
▶FILE *fopen(name, mode)
      char *name;
      char *mode;
```

Opens for buffered reading and/or writing the ASCII or binary file given by name. The selection is given by the string at mode. See your compiler's documentation for a definition of the character strings allowed at mode.

▶int fprintf(fp, ctrl_str, args. . .)
    FILE *fp;
    char *ctrl_str;

args may be of various types, as described by the conversion parameters at ctrl_str. The number of args may vary from none to as many as are practical.

Converts numeric values listed in args to the printable forms according to the conversion specifications given in the string at ctrl_str, and prints this string to the file referenced by fp. Conversion options are described later in printf.

int fputc(c, fp)
    int c;
    FILE *fp;

Writes the character c to stream fp. This function is sometimes used through a macro substitution for the more popular putc(), supplying stdout for fp.

▶int fputs(ptr, fp)
    char *ptr;
    FILE *fp;

Prints the string at ptr to the file referenced by fp.

▶void free(ptr)
    char *ptr;

Releases the memory acquired during a previous calloc, from which ptr was returned. Note that some implementations of this function require that memory be freed in the order in which it was calloced.

▶int ftoa(ptr, dbl, prec, mode)
    char *ptr;
    double dbl;
    int prec;
    int mode;

Converts the dbl into a character string at ptr (make sure there's enough room) according to the precision (how many places significant after the decimal point) and mode given. The mode may be g, e, or f as described later for the printf function.

```
void get(ptr)
        char *ptr;
```

Retrieves characters from the console and places them at ptr up to a newline character. Appends a null before returning.

```
void get_time(ptr)
        char *ptr;
```

Retrieves the system date and time using a PC DOS/MS-DOS interrupt function call. Constructs a string in the form MM/DD/YY HH:MM at ptr.

```
▶int getc(fp)
        FILE *fp;
```

Retrieves one character at a time from the file referenced by fp. Returns EOF at the end of the file, or -1 if an error occurred.

```
▶int getchar()
```

Retrieves one character at a time from the user's console. Note that some compilers actually convert this function into an fgetc with the file referencing the stdin I/O stream.

```
int getnlin(ptr, n)
        char *ptr;
        int n;
```

Retrieves characters from the user's console up to a newline character or until n characters have been seen, and places them at ptr.

```
▶char *gets(buff)
        char *buff;
```

Retrieves characters from the user's console up to a newline character and places them at ptr. Returns the address of buff.

```
int hit(str, c, n)
        char *str[ ];
        char c;
        int n;
```

Returns the array index in str where the character c was found as the first character of the n character strings, or returns -1 if not found (used in menu. c).

```
void h_setup(loc, n, str)
        struct edges loc[ ];
        int n;
        char *str[ ];
```

Figures out how n menu items should be organized horizontally according to parameters included in the array of structures loc. Uses strings at str to calculate space required for each menu item (used in menu. c).

▶int inchar()

Returns a character from the user console without waiting for a newline or echoing. Highly operating system dependent.

```
▶int int86(n, optr, iptr)
        int n;
        struct _regs optr;
        struct _regs iptr;
```

A function that is highly operating system and compiler dependent, which accesses the IBM PC ROM BIOS interrupt functions. This function is used when portability must be sacrificed for performance, as in the function scan(). The interrupt vector number is placed in n, and values for the 8088/8086 AX, BX, and CX registers are placed in the _regs structure pointed to by optr. On return, the iptr structure is filled with the register contents resulting from the function. Returns the value of the flags register.

```
▶isalpha(c)
        int c;
```

Returns TRUE if c is in the range a to z or A to Z, or else FALSE. Sometimes implemented as a macro producing in-line code instead of as a function call.

```
▶isdigit(c)
        int c;
```

Returns TRUE if c is in the range 0 to 9, or else FALSE. Sometimes implemented as a macro producing in-line code instead of as a function call.

```
▶isprint(c)
        int c;
```

Returns TRUE if c is in the range 0x20 (a space) to 0x7e [a tilde (~)], or else FALSE. Sometimes implemented as a macro producing in-line code instead of as a function call.

▶isspace(c)
        int c;

Returns TRUE if c is white space (a space, tab, or newline), or else FALSE. Sometimes implemented as a macro producing in-line code instead of as a function call.

▶char *itoa(ptr, val)
        char *ptr;
        int val;

Converts the integer val into the ASCII string at ptr. (Make sure there's enough room.) Returns the original pointer.

unsigned int jul(date, base)
        char *date;
        int base;

Returns the days from January 1 of the base year up to and including the day given by the date string at date. date is in the form MM/DD/YY or MM-DD-YY.

int keepme(name)
        char *name;

Stores the characters typed at the user console in the file created under the name name up to Ctrl-C. Returns the number of characters stored.

int listme(src, dst)
        char *src;
        char *dst;

Copies the characters from the file with the name at src to the file with the name at dst. If dst is a null string, the file at src is listed on the user's console.

▶double log(val)
        double val;

Returns the common logarithm of val.

▶char *malloc(size)
        unsigned int size;

Returns a pointer to an area of memory size bytes big, or else null. The area reserved is not cleared, as it is for the function calloc().

```
int menu(ptr, hv)
        struct choice ptr[ ];
        int hv;
```

Returns the selection from among menu items described in the array of structures at ptr. A horizontal or vertical arrangement is selected on the screen by giving hv a Ø or 1 value, respectively.

```
void move(dst, src)
        char *dst;
        char *src;
```

Copies the characters from the string at src to the space at dst up to the end of string null at src.

```
void numbers(value, buffer)
        double value;
        char *buffer;
```

Converts the numeric value val into the wordy string at buffer.

```
void outchar(c)
        int c;
```

A function that writes c on the user console without buffering or translation. Highly operating system and compiler dependent.

```
void place(row, col)
        int row;
        int col;
```

Positions the cursor at row, col on the user's console. Note that a #define within the source module allows use with both ANSI and non-ANSI terminals.

```
▶int printf(ctrl_str, args...)
        char *ctrl_str;
```

args may be of various types, as described by the conversion parameters at ctrl_str. The number of args may vary from none to as many as are practical.

Converts numeric values listed in args to the printable forms according to the conversion specifications given in the string at ctrl_str, and prints this string to the user's console (stdout). The following conversion options are available:

%   Indicates that a conversion specification fol-
        lows. Number of inversion specifications
        should be the same as the number of
        arguments.

–   Indicates that the output is to be left-justified

nn   A one- or two-digit decimal value that indi-
        cates the maximum field width; if the value
        has a leading zero, the output will include
        leading zeros; otherwise, the output will in-
        clude spaces (the default).

n. d   Indicates a maximum field width with d digits
        after the decimal point

l   Indicates that the data value is a long int
        rather than an ordinary int

*   Indicates that you use the next value in the
        argument list as a numeric quantity in the
        control string

The following special characters define the end of a conversion
specification element begun with a %:

d   Treats the argument as an int and prints it as
        a decimal number

o   Treats the argument as an int and prints it as
        an octal number

x   Treats the argument as an int and prints it as
        a hexadecimal number

u   Treats the argument as an int and prints it as
        an unsigned decimal number

c   Treats the argument as an int and prints it as
        an ASCII character

s   Treats the argument as a pointer to char and
        prints the string of ASCII characters found
        there up to the null (also converts single
        newline characters—0x0a to carriage re-
        turn/line feed pairs)

e   Treats the argument as a float or double and prints it as a scientific number, with a default precision of 6 digits after the decimal point (may be modified by a leading n. d specifier)

f   Treats the argument as a float or double and prints it in decimal notation, with a default precision of 6 digits after the decimal point (may be changed with a leading n. d specifier)

g   Treats the argument as a float or double and prints it in either decimal or scientific notation, whichever is shorter

All other characters found in the control string are printed as is. See your compiler's documentation for more details and local idiosyncrasies. If no conversion specifications are found, the control string is printed as is.

▶int putc(c, fp)
        int c;
        FILE *fp;

Writes the character c on the stream *fp. Depending on the mode in which the stream was opened (ASCII or binary), the function translates newline characters (\n). Returns the character c.

▶putchar(c)
        int c;

Writes the character c to stdout. Sometimes converted by a macro to the equivalent putc(c, stdout). Returns c.

▶int puts(ptr)
        char *ptr;

Prints the string at ptr to the user's console with a trailing newline character (frequently converted to carriage return/line feed).

void report(info)
        struct info_block *info;

Prepares a report where data referenced within the structure info is printed in columns with headers and with so many columns per page. On the last page the columns are footed.

void reprint(n)
        int n;

Reprints an entry window given by the nth element of the array of structures used to define the entry fields (used in scan.c).

```
char *revjul(jul, year)
        int jul;
        int year;
```

Returns a pointer to a date string, given a Julian date and base year.

```
void say(ptr)
        char *ptr;
```

Prints the string at ptr on the user's console.

```
int scan(ptr)
        struct _scan *ptr;
```

Implements the features of the dBASE II function:

@ row,col say "string" get variable picture "mask"

scan() gets passed a pointer to an array of structures that define what to do and where to do it. See the function and its accompanying documentation for a complete description.

```
▶int scanf(ctrl_str, args...)
        char *ctrl_str;
```

args may be of various types, as described by the conversion parameters at ctrl_str. The number of args may vary from none to as many as are practical.

Retrieves input from the user console (stdin) and attempts to convert the input according to the specifications in ctrl_str and to place the resulting values in the addresses pointed to by args. (Thus, all the args are pointer values.) The conversion specifications are similar to those for printf and include the following:

%	Indicates that a conversion specification follows
l	Treat the argument as a long int rather than a normal int
d	A decimal integer
o	An octal integer
x	A hexadecimal integer
h	A short integer

c A single ASCII character

s A character string

f A floating-point number (float or double)

Leading white space is generally ignored but delimits multiple entries from one another. The function returns one of the following: (1) -1 if end of file is reached (a result that can be obtained if input is redirected from the user's console at run time); (2) zero if no arguments can be converted; or (3) the number of successful conversions. See your compiler's documentation for more details and local idiosyncrasies.

```
void scroll(dir, row, col, max, width)
        int dir;
        unsigned int row, col;
        int max, width;
```

A function (for IBM PCs and compatibles) to roll the contents of a window on the user's console defined by its upper left corner (row and col) and the width and number of lines deep (max). dir determines whether to scroll the window from the bottom up or vice versa. The empty line created is filled with spaces. Used with window().

```
void set_cursor(flag)
        int flag;
```

A function (for IBM PC and compatibles) to turn the cursor on and off or just to reshape the cursor.

```
▶void setmem(ptr, size, value)
        char *ptr;
        unsigned int size;
        int value;
```

Fills the area of memory pointed to by ptr with value for size bytes.

```
int shl_string(s, insert, limit)
        char *s;
        char insert;
        char limit;
```

Shifts left the non-white-space contents of the string at s into white space by one character and stops at the limit character (which may be a null), then inserts insert in front of the limit character.

Returns TRUE if white space existed into which the string could be moved; otherwise, the function returns FALSE.

```
void shr_string(s, limit)
      char *s;
      int limit;
```

Shifts right the non-white-space contents of the string at s, stopping at the limit character (which may be a null), prepending a space.

```
int sindex(ptr, c)
      char *ptr;
      int c;
```

Attempts to find the character c in the string at ptr. Returns the offset into the string where the character was found, or -1 if not found.

```
▶int sizeof(x)
      x is a variable type
```

Not a function at all but a compile-time operation that "returns" the size in bytes of the variable acted on.

```
▶sprintf(ptr, ctrl_str, args. . . )
      char *ptr;
      char *ctrl_str;
```

args may be of various types, as described by the conversion parameters at ctrl_str. The number of args may vary from none to as many as are practical.

Similar to printf but prints output at the place pointed to by ptr. (See printf for a description of other parameters.)

```
▶char *strcat(dst, src)
      char *dst;
      char *src;
```

Concatenates the string at src onto the end of the string at dst. The null at the end of the original dst string is replaced by the first character of the src string. Be sure to allow enough room at dst for the resulting longer string.

```
▶char *strchr(ptr, c)
      char *ptr;
      int c;
```

Returns a pointer to the first occurrence of c found in the string at ptr, or else a null.

▶ int strcmp(ptr1, ptr2)
    char *ptr1;
    char *ptr2;

Returns the result of subtracting, one character at a time, the string at ptr2 from ptr1. A negative result indicates that string 1 has character values lower than string 2, a positive value indicates that string 1 values are greater than those of string 2, and a zero result indicates that the values are the same.

▶ char *strcpy(ptr1, ptr2)
    char *ptr1;
    char *ptr2;

Copies the string at ptr2 to the place pointed to by ptr1 up to the end-of-string null at string 2.

▶ int strlen(ptr)
    char *ptr;

Returns the length of the string at ptr.

▶ char *strncpy(ptr1, ptr2, n)
    char *ptr1;
    char *ptr2;
    int n;

Copies the string at ptr2 to the place pointed to by ptr1 for n-1 characters or until the end-of-string null at string 2. Always appends a null at string 1.

void toggle(ptr, str, lft, rt, flag)
    struct edges *ptr;
    int flag;
    char *lft;
    char *rt;
    char *str;

Writes a string at str on the user's console at locations defined in the structure at *ptr with left and right video attributes given by the strings at *lft and *rt (ANSI control sequences). flag determines whether the left attribute will actually be placed in front of the string, resulting in the attribute being turned on or off.

```
void toggle_attributes(flag, n)
        int flag;
        int n;
```

Turns on or off (according to the value of flag) the optional video attributes on either side of a display window defined by the nth array of structures for input fields (used in scan. c).

```
int twodates(str1, str2)
        char *str1;
        char *str2;
```

Returns the days between the two date strings given at str1 and str2.

```
void update(n)
        int n;
```

Prints the numeric value in the display window as defined by the nth array of structures for input fields (used in scan. c).

```
void v_setup(loc, n, str)
        struct edges loc[ ];
        int n;
        char *str[ ];
```

Figures out how n menu items should be organized vertically according to parameters included in the array of structures loc. Uses strings at str to calculate space required for each (used in menu. c).

```
void window(row, col, width, max, dir, line)
        int row;
        int col;
        int width;
        int max;
        int dir;
        char *line[ ];
```

Manages display of character strings from the array line on a window defined by row and col positions on the user's console, max characters wide. Newlines are placed at either the top or the bottom, and scrolling occurs in the direction defined by dir.

```
char *zeller(date)
        char *date;
```

Returns a pointer to string, such as "Monday", "Tuesday", etc., from the date string at date in the form MM-DD-YY or MM/DD/YY.

```
int _atoi(ptr)
       char *ptr;
```

Simple-minded ASCII-to-integer conversion function that returns the integer value of the string at ptr.

```
char *_itoa(ptr, n)
       char *ptr;
       int n;
```

Simple-minded integer-to-ASCII conversion function that places the converted n into the numeric string at ptr, returning the original ptr.

Index

More Computer Knowledge from Que

LOTUS SOFTWARE TITLES

1-2-3 for Business	$16.95
1-2-3 Financial Macros	19.95
1-2-3 Macro Library	19.95
1-2-3 Tips, Tricks, and Traps	16.95
Using 1-2-3	17.95
Using 1-2-3 Workbook and Disk	29.95
Using Jazz	19.95
Using Symphony	19.95
Symphony: Advanced Topics	19.95
Symphony Macros and the Command Language	18.95
Symphony Tips, Tricks, and Traps	19.95

WORD-PROCESSING TITLES

Improve Your Writing with Word Processing	12.95
Using DisplayWrite	16.95
Using Microsoft Word	16.95
Using MultiMate	16.95
Using the PFS Family: FILE, WRITE, GRAPH, REPORT	14.95
Using WordPerfect	16.95
Using WordStar 2000	17.95

IBM TITLES

IBM PC Expansion & Software Guide	21.95
IBM's Personal Computer, 2nd Edition	17.95
Networking IBM PCs: A Practical Guide	18.95
PC DOS User's Guide	16.95
PC DOS Workbook	14.95
Real Managers Use Personal Computers!	14.95

APPLICATIONS SOFTWARE TITLES

dBase III Advanced Programming	19.95
dBase III Handbook	17.95
Multiplan Models for Business	15.95
Spreadsheet Software: From VisiCalc to 1-2-3	15.95
SuperCalc SuperModels for Business	16.95
Using AppleWorks	16.95
Using Enable	17.95
Using Dollars and Sense	14.95
VisiCalc Models for Business	16.95

COMPUTER SYSTEMS TITLES

MS-DOS User's Guide	16.95
The HP Touchscreen	19.95
The HP 110 Portable: Power to Go!	16.95
Using NetWare	24.95

PROGRAMMING AND TECHNICAL TITLES

Advanced C: Techniques and Applications	19.95
Common C Functions	17.95
C Programmer's Library	19.95
C Programming Guide, 2nd Edition	19.95
CP/M Programmer's Encyclopedia	19.95
CP/M Software Finder	14.95
C Self-Study Guide	16.95
Turbo Pascal for BASIC Programmers	14.95
Understanding UNIX: A Conceptual Guide	19.95
Understanding XENIX: A Conceptual Guide	19.95

Que Order Line: **1-800-428-5331**

All prices subject to change without notice.

LEARN MORE ABOUT C
WITH THESE OUTSTANDING BOOKS FROM QUE

C Self-Study Guide
by Jack Purdum

This self-directed study guide uses a unique question-and-answer format to take you through the basics and into advanced areas of the C programming language. The book includes complete programs for testing new functions and for illustrating tips, traps, techniques, and shortcuts. A perfect companion for the *C Programming Guide*, this book will help you teach yourself to program in C. A companion disk is available.

C Programming Guide, 2nd Edition
by Jack Purdum

Keep up-to-date on the latest developments in the C programming language with this revised edition of the best-selling *C Programming Guide*. This popular tutorial shows you the secrets of experts—the tips, tricks, and techniques that take so long to learn on your own. Gain the knowledge and skill you need to venture into all areas of programming, from operating systems to accounting packages, with this highly respected book.

Common C Functions
by Kim J. Brand

This book displays dozens of C functions that are designed to teach C coding techniques to provide useful building blocks for program development. Learn the elements and structures of C programming by studying C code written by others. If you want to gain a stronger understanding of C code and how it works, *Common C Functions* is a superb guide. All the C code in this book is available on disk.

C Programmer's Library
by Jack Purdum, Timothy Leslie, and Alan Stegemoller

The most advanced book about C on the market today, this best-seller will save you hours of programming time and help you write more efficient code. Author Jack Purdum discusses design considerations in writing programs and offers programming tips to help you take full advantage of the power of C. A disk containing all the programs in the book is available.

Item	Title	Price	Quantity	Extension
176	C Self-Study Guide	$ 16.95		
284	Companion Disk, IBM PC format	39.95		
285	Companion Disk, 8-inch SS/SD	39.95		
148	Common C Functions	17.95		
280	Companion Disk, IBM PC format	49.95		
281	Companion Disk, 8-inch SS/SD	49.95		
188	C Programming Guide, 2nd Edition	19.95		
45	C Programmer's Library	19.95		
270	Companion Disk, IBM PC format	124.95		
271	Companion Disk, 8-inch SS/SD	124.95		

Book Subtotal	
Shipping & Handling ($1.75 per item)	
Indiana Residents Add 5% Sales Tax	
GRAND TOTAL	

Method of Payment:

☐ Check ☐ VISA ☐ MasterCard ☐ American Express

Card Number _____ Exp. Date _____

Cardholder Name _____

Ship to _____

Address _____

City _____ State _____ ZIP _____

If you can't wait, call **1-800-428-5331** and order TODAY.

All prices subject to change without notice.

CCF-8510